Django Reinhardt

KNOW THE MAN, PLAY THE MUSIC

Dave Gelly & Rod Fogg

Django Reinhardt

Dave Gelly & Rod Fogg

A BACKBEAT BOOK
First edition 2005
Published by Backbeat Books
600 Harrison Street
San Francisco, CA 94107, US
www.backbeatbooks.com

An imprint of The Music Player Network, United Entertainment Media Inc.

Published for Backbeat Books by Outline Press Ltd,
2A Union Court, 20-22 Union Road, London SW4 6JP, England
www.backbeatuk.com

ISBN 0-879308-37-0

EDITOR John Morrish
DESIGN Paul Cooper Design

Printed by SNP Excel (China) Company Ltd.

05 06 07 08 09 5 4 3 2 1

Contents

Django Reinhardt

THE LIFE

Gipsy Roots

IT IS EASY TO FIND THE SMALL Belgian town of Liberchies, sometimes spelt 'Liverchies'. It is close to exit 21 on autoroute A54, just north of Charleroi. Indeed, if it were much closer it would be in the middle of exit 21. But you will search in vain for the birthplace of Django Reinhardt. He was born on January 23rd 1910, in a Gipsy encampment on the edge of town. A few days later he was gone. It is unlikely that he ever revisited the place.

His mother, one of a band of itinerant Gipsy entertainers, danced and performed acrobatics under the name of La Belle Laurence. His father is believed to have been one Jean Vées (or 'Weiss'), a clown, musician and repairer of musical instruments, but La Belle Laurence was an independent woman. She kept to her family name of Reinhardt and passed it on to her son. He was named Jean-Baptiste and given the pet name 'Django'. Nicknames were common among these people. Django's mother was generally known as 'Négros', because of her dark complexion, and his younger brother, Joseph, was dubbed 'Nin-Nin', for reasons that no-one could remember.

The Gipsies are an ancient people, whose origins lie in the Indian sub-continent. At some time during their wanderings, a diaspora occured. One branch, the Manouche, entered western Europe from the Middle East via the Balkans and Hungary; the other, the Gitanes, via southern Europe and Spain. The Reinhardts were Manouche. They had been travelling around

> He was named Jean-Baptiste and given the pet name 'Django'

Belgium and northern France for several decades, having drifted there from Germany after the Franco-Prussian war of 1870. It was a part of the world that had been fought over repeatedly, and was soon to be fought over again. Travel 50 km north from Liberchies and you arrive at the site of the Battle of Waterloo. Travel 50 km west and you find yourself at the ill-fated town of Mons. World War I broke out when Django was aged four, and the territory over which his mother's little band of entertainers had plied their trade became one huge battlefield, the Western Front.

Blown by the winds of conflict, the Gipsies headed south, along the Côte d'Azur, into Italy, across to Corsica and finally as far as Algiers. In 1919, following the Armistice, they retraced their steps and made for Paris, planting themselves amidst the sprawling shantytown of 'roulottes' (caravans) and shacks that clustered around the Porte de Choisy, on the southern edge of the city. This is where Django grew up.

Life in the Gipsy settlement could be portrayed in various ways. Looked at from one angle it was a grubby, poverty-stricken, hand-to-mouth existence, in which children were left to fend for themselves and drift into fecklessness and crime. Another observer might depict it as a free-and-easy affair, with few responsibilities or obligations, and a veritable paradise for children, who could do whatever they liked with minimal adult interference. Django's experience seems to have been more like the latter. His principal activities

Django at 13 with his banjo-guitar

consisted of fighting, stealing coal from horse-drawn wagons, going to the cinema and learning to play billiards for money. His formal education lasted exactly one day, with the result that he passed his entire life as a functional illiterate. The thing that set him apart from the other kids, however, was his utter intoxication with music.

Django was the child of a culture in which every social occasion was accompanied by music. Wherever it was being played, he would be there. He would leave his friends and sit, transfixed by the sound of it. His powers of concentration where music was concerned were formidable and he seemed quite oblivious to his surroundings while it was being played. He longed for an instrument of his own, but there was no chance that his mother would buy him one, even if she could have afforded it.

Finally, when Django was just 12, a neighbour gave him an old banjo-guitar, a hybrid, six-stringed instrument, tuned like a guitar but with the body of a banjo. Lacking a teacher, Django would watch men playing, memorise their fingering and practise at home. He would spend whole days at this, trying to reproduce what he had heard. It was common, in his world, for boys to spend idle hours picking out tunes on whatever instruments happened to be at hand. No-one paid much attention to Django's single-minded devotion to the banjo-guitar, except to tell him to shut up when somebody was trying to sleep. Even then, Django would sleep with the instrument beside him.

His father, Jean Vées, and an uncle played regularly at a cafe near the Porte de Clignancourt. To listen to them play, Django would creep into the room and hide under a table. His uncle eventually discovered him and asked what he was doing. "Just listening," replied Django, admitting that he was teaching himself to play.

His uncle handed him his guitar, saying, "All right. Let's hear what you can do." The result astonished everyone present. The boy already had the makings of a mature and confident musician. He was recruited into the family business on the spot and his professional career began. Before long, he was working independently of his relatives, playing in a dance-hall with the popular accordionist Guérino. He was still only 12 years old. At the end of each night's work his mother would arrive to collect him, not to guard him from the dangers of night-time Paris – he was already streetwise far beyond his years – but to relieve him of his takings. Even at this tender age Django showed clear symptoms of being a compulsive gambler.

What sort of music was he playing? Well, it certainly wasn't jazz. This was 1922 or 1923, and, although the term 'jazz' was becoming fashionable, nobody had much idea about what it actually meant, beyond youthful rebellion, peppy music and having a good time. American troops had brought a kind of jazzy ragtime to Europe towards the end of the war, followed in 1919 by Will Marion Cook's Southern Syncopated Orchestra, starring Sidney Bechet. American songs were quite popular, too. Django's French biographer, Charles Delaunay, mentions 'Dinah' and 'The Sheik Of Araby' as two such tunes that he often played at this time. He liked to hang around outside a club in the Place Pigalle, entranced by the music of Billy Arnold's Novelty Jazz Band. But most of the music he played would have been earthy local dance music, the majority in a lively, thumping waltz-time. The most common instruments were accordion, banjo and violin.

And what sort of place did the boy Django play in? Mainly cafes and the species of dance-hall known as 'bal-musette'. Delaunay describes these as "meeting places of thieves, spivs and prostitutes", and goes on to provide the following sketch:

"The bal-musette! The very name conjures up visions of smoky dance-halls with carved mirrors, the tables and walls inscribed with intertwined initials or naive scribblings that could be made out by the glow of unshaded red light bulbs hanging from the ceiling. The band had to climb up a vertical ladder to reach a tiny projecting balcony. After each set a musician made a collection with the time-honoured, 'Your loose change in the hat, please!' These things are representative of a whole era, a whole social milieu. Right-thinking people never ventured into such dangerous company, unless they were out for a cheap thrill."

Anyone familiar with the red-light district memoirs of early New Orleans jazz musicians will instantly recognise the picture. Similar scenes could have been found at the time in most big cities and seaports. Jazz, bal-musette, tango, flamenco, fado – these all developed at around the same time and share very similar origins.

Django's reputation among musicians grew steadily during his early teens. He won a prize for his banjo playing and worked a summer season with the accordionist Jean

A portrait of the artiste as a young man.

Vaissade at a resort near Le Touquet. He was in great demand, but easily became bored with playing regularly in the the same place, with the same people.

After the first week, he would often begin sending other players, usually from his own close-knit circle, to take his place. Bandleaders became resigned to having one or other of Django's 'cousins' turn up. Vaissade used to claim that he had eventually shared the stage with the entire Reinhardt / Vées clan.

At the age of 17, Django married a girl, Bella Baumgartner, from the same Gipsy settlement. The marriage took place according to tradition. The young couple eloped and stayed away for a few days. When they returned they were regarded as man and wife and their union was sealed by a celebration with music and dancing.

The following year saw Django's recording debut, still playing banjo, with Vaissade. He even had his name on the record label, although it appeared as 'Jiango Renard', because he was unable to spell it out. The next attempt emerged as 'Jeangot'. He made four recording sessions in 1928, two with Vaissade, one with another accordionist, Marceau, and one with the singer Chaumel. Their only value nowadays is as curiosities, especially since on eight of the 16 numbers the featured instrument is a swanee whistle.

Nevertheless, the name of Django Reinhardt, however it was spelt, was being passed around. It came to the ears of the English bandleader and impressario Jack Hylton, leader of perhaps the most polished and fashionable dance orchestra in Europe and sometimes referred to as 'Britain's Paul Whiteman'.

The immaculate Hylton, in full evening dress, complete with cigar and attended by two exquisite young women, turned up one night at La Java, a dive where Django was appearing. Highly impressed, Hylton offered Django a job on the spot, and Django accepted. How long he would have stuck to it, and how Hylton would have reacted when the inevitable parade of cousins began showing up, is an interesting speculation. As things turned out, Django couldn't take the job. A few days later he almost died, and his life changed forever.

Out of the fire

DJANGO'S YOUNG WIFE, BELLA, practised the traditional Gipsy craft of making artificial flowers. She would spend evenings at this task while Django was out playing, and when he came home in the early hours the caravan would be piled high with pretty confections of paper and celluloid. On the night of November 2nd 1928, Django returned home and made his way to bed through the heaps of flowers. As he did so he thought he heard a scrabbling noise, possibly a mouse. He picked up the candle to investigate. It slipped from his fingers and fell among the flowers. There was an instant conflagration. Django grabbed a blanket in an attempt to smother the flames, but it was no use. By the time his neighbours had dragged him free of the blazing caravan Django was in a bad way. They rushed him to Lariboisière, a charity hospital, where it was found that his right leg was very badly burned, while his left hand was virtually unrecognisable as a hand at all.

The doctors advised amputating the leg, but Django resisted. Fearful that the authorities might ignore his pleas, his relatives removed him from the hospital and carried him back to his father-in-law's caravan. It was obvious that Django would need proper medical care, so they pooled their money to pay for a private nursing home. Once there, his leg began to heal slowly and after about 18 months he could get about with the aid of a stick. Eventually, by sheer persistence, he was able to walk normally. But the left hand, the one with which he fingered the fretboard, was another matter entirely. It was so badly scarred that the

> It seemed that Django would never play a stringed instrument again

third and fourth fingers were bent and paralysed, and no amount of willpower would ever restore them to working order. It seemed that Django would never play a stringed instrument again.

What prompted his cousins to bring him a guitar is unclear. Some say the doctors recommended it as a form of therapy, to help him recover as much digital mobility as possible. Others claim that the Gipsies believed supernatural powers would intervene. It may well be that Django simply made up his mind to overcome this handicap and refused to accept that it was impossible. Whatever the case, he now set about devising a method of playing the guitar with a thumb, two good fingers and two virtually dead ones.

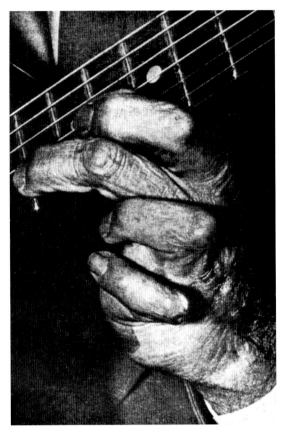

Django's left hand: a thumb, two good fingers and two that were virtually dead.

He devoted the same degree of concentration to this task as he had to teaching himself the banjo-guitar as a child. In a remarkably short time he was limping around the streets of Montmartre, serenading the café terraces with love-songs before passing the hat around.

Other musicians watched, astounded, as Django's new technique quickly developed. He had now abandoned the old, hybrid banjo-guitar in favour of the guitar proper, an altogether more serious instrument. Along with his self-devised technique, a new and highly personal style was beginning to emerge. He was mixing, too, with a more sophisticated crowd of musicians than those he had worked with in the bals-musette. In particular he liked to visit the Can-Can, a musicians' hangout in Pigalle. Here his playing received knowledgeable appreciation and he was also able to hear some of the best jazz-influenced musicians that France had to offer. Among them was the pianist Stéphane Mougin, who asked him to join his band at Les Acacias at the sizeable salary of 100 francs a night. Django's rehabilitation was complete and, as 1930 drew to a close, his true artistic career had begun.

Django's wife, Bella, had been badly traumatised by the caravan fire. She had escaped, but with her hair ablaze. She had also been pregnant and in due course gave birth to a son, Henri, who took his mother's family name of Baumgartner. Henri Baumgartner, universally known by his nickname, 'Lousson', also grew up to play the guitar. He died in 1992, aged 63. Bella and Django never lived together again after the fire. He now formed a liaison with one of his many cousins, Sophie Ziegler, known as 'Naguine'.

After a while, Django and Naguine set off for the south, with the vague idea of living it up on the Côte d'Azur, the playground of the rich. Django's younger brother, Joseph ('Nin-Nin'), himself a very competent guitarist, went with them. It was a hand-to-mouth existence, mostly playing in bars for tips and drinks. The obvious question is why a man capable of earning 100 francs a night in Paris should go wandering about the French countryside with no idea where his next meal might come from. The answer is that Django Reinhardt conducted his entire life on impulse and was impervious to what most people would call common sense. He seemed to have no concept of the value of money and spent or gave away whatever he happened to have in his pocket. One minute he was living a life of luxury, the next minute he was broke. He accepted both circumstances with equal indifference. Money was not something one earned – indeed, he despised people who worked for wages, calling them 'peasants' – and it was certainly not something one saved. Money was for gambling with, for cutting a dash with, for playing the lavish host with. His attitude to life drove other people mad with frustration, but there was nothing they could do about it.

The little party drifted, mostly on foot, from Nice to Cannes and on to Toulon. There they wandered into the Café des Lions, where Django and Joseph played for a while, passed the hat for few francs, scored a free drink and a sandwich each and left. Just another stop along the way. But they had been overheard. Lodging in a room above the bar was Émile Savitry, one of those bohemian men-about-the-arts that only France seems able to produce. A photographer, traveller, friend of the avant-garde and lover of jazz, Savitry had recently returned from the South Seas and was considering how to occupy himself from now on. At first Savitry thought that the music downstairs sounded so good it must be coming from the radio or a record. By the time he came to investigate, the guitarists had gone.

Brothers: Joseph and Django with clarinettist Gérard Lévêque in 1938.

After much searching, Savitry found Django and Joseph in a bar, playing billiards and minus instruments. Having borrowed a couple of guitars and persuaded the brothers to play for him, he was vastly impressed. He asked them if they listened to much jazz, to which they gave vague, non-committal answers, and invited them to his apartment above the Café des Lions to listen to some records.

That afternoon proved to be a turning point in Django's musical life. This was the first time he had heard the foremost American exponents of the new musical art – Eddie Lang, Joe Venuti, Duke Ellington, and especially Louis Armstrong. The beauty of the young Armstrong's trumpet playing reduced him to tears and he was heard to murmur "mon frère" ("my brother"). Savitry had to go away for a few days. In an act of heroic generosity, he handed Django the key to his apartment, telling him to make himself at home and enjoy the music. When he returned he found not only Django, Joseph and Naguine in residence, but also Négros, who had turned up from Paris to make sure her boys were safe and well. For a while she cooked and kept house for all five of them.

Savitry fixed the brothers a week's engagement at Le Coq Hardy, a smartish restaurant and nightclub, and bought them dinner-jackets to wear. At the end of the week Django's pockets were full of cash, enough to last a prudent man several weeks. He spent it all on a feast in Savitry's honour. "Tomorrow," he declared, "we begin again!"

And quite soon another stroke of luck came his way. Louis Vola, who played accordion, guitar and double bass, was putting together a small group to play in the new Boîte à Matelots bar at the Palm Beach club in Cannes. Quite by chance, he heard the brothers playing on the seafront and invited them to join. He discovered that Django and Naguine were staying at the George V, the most expensive hotel in town. Django could put on a convincing aristocratic manner when called upon, and they had simply walked in and booked a room. Vola thought that the management had taken him for "a Hindu prince". Vola settled the bill and set them up in a little bungalow next to his own, near the Palm Beach.

The engagement went very well, with Vola keeping a close eye on Django to ensure that he didn't wander off. However, the presence of Django acted like a magnet, attracting first his extended family, then his friends and finally what seemed like half the Manouche travellers in France. The little bungalow was overflowing with cousins, others parked their caravans in the road outside, and the throng gradually spread throughout the neighbourhood. Eventually, the Mayor of Cannes implored Vola to do something about it. By this time the end of the season had arrived, the Boîte à Matelots job finished

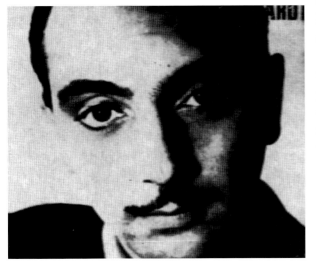

Magnetic personality: Django in 1933.

and they all melted away. When they had gone the Palm Beach discovered that it was mysteriously short of cutlery and table-linen.

Django returned to Paris, where he and his family descended on Savitry in his studio, proceeding to colonise it just as they had colonised his Toulon apartment. Savitry revelled in their chaotic company, and was quite sorry when they eventually returned to their old home at Porte de Choisy. He was later to take some of the best and most characteristic photographic portraits of Django.

Django's playing came to the ears of the singer Jean Sablon, sometimes called 'the French Bing Crosby'. Indeed, his relaxed style had a distinctly American rhythmic feel about it. Many of Crosby's early recordings benefited greatly from the swinging guitar of Eddie Lang in the accompaniment and Sablon no doubt envisaged a similar role for Django. The problem was holding onto him. A system was evolved whereby the saxophonist André Ekyan would pick Django up in Sablon's car, drive him to rehearsals and drive him home afterwards. This meant that Sablon rarely saw his own car, but he obviously considered it worth the sacrifice.

Sablon was now becoming a big star, and Django toured widely with his band through 1933 and 1934. It opened up a whole new world to him, one to which he had to adapt, but in which he never felt entirely comfortable. Travelling involved alien items like clocks and timetables, and it sometimes meant filling out forms, which someone else had to do for him. When it came to appearing in London, Django at first refused either to fly or travel by boat. "There are spies," he said darkly, but declined to explain further.

Eventually he gave in and agreed to fly. He was photographed, with Sablon and members of the band, beneath the wing of a DeHaviland Rapide of Hillman Airways Ltd at Croydon Aerodrome.

From this period it becomes a little easier to follow his movements, because this was when he began recording regularly, and the details of recording sessions are known. And it is on Sablon's records from this period that we first pick up the recognisable sound of Django Reinhardt's guitar. There are brief solos and snatches of accompaniment from him on such early tracks as 'Je Suis Sex-Appeal' (March 1933) and 'Le Jour Ou Je Te Vis' (January 1934). They reveal that the firm rhythmic grasp and clean, incisive phrasing that were abiding characteristics of his style were now well and truly in place. The last-named piece has a special significance in Django's story, because it comes from the first recording session with his future musical partner, Stéphane Grappelli.

A little orchestra

AT FIRST GLANCE, IT WOULD BE DIFFICULT to find a more ill-matched pair than Stéphane Grappelli and Django Reinhardt. Grappelli was born in 1908, the son of a cultured but impecunious Italian immigrant father, a freelance journalist, and a French mother who had died when when Grappelli was a small child. His fragmented upbringing had included a period at the boarding school run by the dancer Isadora Duncan, her 'Temple of the Dance of the Future'. He taught himself both violin and piano and later attended the Paris Conservatoire. Throughout his early youth he was grindingly poor and earned his living mainly by busking in courtyards and on café terraces. Later, he played piano for the silent cinema. The experience of genteel poverty had the effect of making him very careful with money, always eager to please, and circumspect in his business dealings. Not a great socialiser, he tended to keep to himself.

The effect of jazz on this cautious and buttoned-up youth was cataclysmic. "As soon as I heard it, I understood that it was truly *my* music. Jazz seemed to have been invented expressly for me." As with Django, it was Armstrong who had the greatest effect on him: "Louis Armstrong with two notes could make you cry." Armstrong and jazz, he said towards the end of his long life, "changed my destiny". Although it was not possible to play real jazz for a living, Grappelli did well from playing the kind of novelty pseudo-jazz that was all the rage in 1920s Paris. Eventually he joined France's top show band, Grégor and his Gregorians, playing both violin and piano, plus a bit of saxophone and accordion, with dancing the Charleston as a sideline. With the Gregorians he travelled widely, even as far as Argentina. It was during these travels that Grappelli began spelling his name 'Grappelly', a form that he retained throughout much of his career. He did it, he said, because in Anglophone countries people tended to pronounce it 'Grappell-eye'. When Grégor got into a spot of trouble with the law and bolted to South America, Grappelli joined André Ekyan's band, playing for Paris society.

A favourite engagement was Le Croix du Sud, the kind of high-bohemian nightclub where the Prince Of Wales had been known to drop in and take a turn playing the drums. How Django came to be there is anyone's guess, but one night Stéphane looked up to find himself being stared at in a disconcerting way by a character who "looked like a gangster straight out of an American film". To Stéphane's disquiet, the apparition approached. He said that he was a musician too, a guitarist, and was looking for a violinist who played jazz to join him in starting "a little orchestra" composed entirely of stringed instruments – "no drums, no trumpets". Since Django had a guitar with him, the only course was to invite him to sit in. Stéphane was "incredibly fascinated by the style of this young Gipsy, who dominated the guitar so well that Paganini would have been pleased to listen". Django seemed equally impressed by Stéphane.

Grappelli was torn. All his musical instincts urged him to throw in his lot with Django there and then, and set up the "little orchestra". But caution told him to stick with the steady job and the regular income provided by Ekyan. Furthermore, even on this brief acquaintance it was pretty clear that Django would not make the easiest of partners. So he didn't join Django in his scheme, but they kept in touch. Django would sit in at the Croix du Sud from time to time, and they would talk about music and their favourite jazz records. Then came the night when Grappelli paid a visit to Django's caravan at Porte de Choisy: "We ate, we smoked and we drank, and of course there was always a violin in the corner." They played duets for the first time. A musical bond between them was instantly forged, but Stéphane still did not feel ready to make a leap in the dark and take matters further. Django, of course was still playing for Jean Sablon, and the next time the two got together was at the recording session of January 15th 1934, already referred to.

> It was clear that Django would not make the easiest of partners

It was Django who first attracted the notice of true jazz enthusiasts. In 1933 the first association of French jazz lovers, a small but committed body, was launched, calling itself the Hot Club de France. It published its own magazine, *Jazz Tango Dancing*, and put on occasional concerts. The ever-helpful Emile Savitry invited the club's Pierre Nourry to his studio to hear Django play. Nourry was so impressed that he arranged for Django to appear at a concert on February 4th 1934. The show was a triumph. The club magazine called him "the revelation of the concert", and went on, "We now have a great improviser in Paris."

Later that year, Django and Stéphane were again thrown together when Louis Vola hired both of them to play in a genteel tea-dance band he had contracted to lead at the Hotel Claridge. The job only took up two hours a day, from five to seven, and even that time was shared with a tango band.

It is the habit of musicians to repair to the nearest bar during intervals, and that's what Vola's men did, all except Django. He took himself off into the bandroom, behind a heavy, sound-deadening curtain, and played the guitar for his own amusement. He rarely felt relaxed in non-Gipsy social situations, and once he had picked up the guitar he was reluctant to put it down. One day, Stephane remained behind with him and they began playing together. It felt so good that they did the same the next day, and every day after that. Vola joined them on bass and Roger Chaput added a second guitar part.

This quartet became a kind of secret society. Its four members played purely in private, for their own enjoyment. As well as during intermissions at the Hotel Claridge, they got together late at night after finishing whatever work they had been doing. They feared that if they made it into a public entertainment the fun and spontaneity of their music would evaporate, and they might be put under pressure to alter their style or to play the latest hits. The quartet grew to a quintet when Django pointed out that, when Grappelli was soloing he had two guitars and bass to back him up, whereas his own solos had the support of only one guitar and bass. Joseph Reinhardt was accordingly added to the strength.

Pierre Nourry and his Hot Club colleague Charles Delaunay visited the Hotel Claridge and were permitted to enter the bandroom sanctum to listen to the music. They recognised at once that here was something entirely new in jazz, something distinctive created by French musicians. They were, in any case, on the lookout for a group to act as the club's house band, and this could be it. Delaunay hit upon the idea of launching the band, not with a live show, but a record. He sold the idea to the Odeon label, but the company rejected the results of the first session, featuring American singer Bert Marshall, as "too modern". He then tried Ultraphone, who accepted and recorded four numbers by the quintet in December 1934.

Even today, those four pieces ('Dinah', 'Tiger Rag', 'Lady Be Good', 'I Saw Stars') come across as uniquely fresh and exciting. The musicians were certainly delighted with them. They must have been exactly what Django had first imagined a "little orchestra without drums or trumpets" would sound like. Dedicated jazz lovers certainly recognised the creative originality and high spirits of the band's music, although the Odeon executive who dismissed it as "too modern" was probably closer to the taste of the general public at the time. Take the first two choruses of the very first number, 'Dinah', which are Django all the way. Part of their beauty comes from the delightful game of hide-and-seek which he plays with the tune. If you know 'Dinah', then you can recognise the brief flashes of it that appear in the first 32 bars, but it is by no means a faithful rendition of the melody as sung by Bing Crosby on his 1932 hit record. In the second chorus Django drops all reference to the original tune and constructs a whole new edifice on the harmonies, voicing the third eight bars (the 'middle eight', or 'release') in octaves. This was an effect which no other jazz guitarist had ever fully exploited, and few would take it up until Wes Montgomery, 30 years later. Stéphane enters at the third chorus, swinging blithely. Going into the fourth and final chorus he is propelled forward by a mightly roll from Django's guitar and piles on the pressure until a quiet coda brings the piece to a calm ending.

It may have been 'modern' and a little challenging on first hearing, but the Quintette began with several advantages. It was easy on the ear, not loud and raucous, which was how most people perceived jazz at the time; Django himself was a spectacular virtuoso, the more so because of his disability, the sound was totally new, which helped the band become fashionable – and, of course, it was French. Hitherto, most French jazz

Awkward in social situations, Django would take himself off and play for his own amusement.

enthusiasts had regarded jazz as a purely American (predominantly black American) phenomenon. Now France had its very own brand of 'le jazz hot'. To this day there is a tacit assumption in French jazz circles that black Americans and Frenchmen make the best jazz musicians.

On the record label, and for its debut concert at L'École Normale de Musique, the band was billed as Django Reinhardt et le Quintette du Hot Club de France avec Stéphane Grappelli, not a snappy title, admittedly, but there was a reason for it. The whole question of who was named, and in which order, had become a diplomatic minefield. At the very beginning, Django was the better known of the two, because of his Hot Club concert and subsequent write-up in the club magazine. On the other hand, Stéphane had been there from the start and considered the Quintette as a joint venture. ("We were partners," he used to say in later years, "like Marks and Spencer.") It was a touchy subject with both of them. Stéphane saw it as a question of publicity and career advancement, whereas to Django it involved dignity and status, a serious

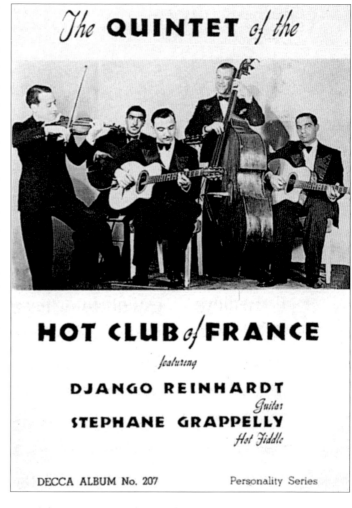

The Quintette began recording for British Decca in 1938.

matter in his culture. Once, when a compère got the words wrong and announced "Stéphane Grappelli et son Quintette", Django stalked off the stage before the first note had been played.

By common consent, the Quintette's records actually increased the following for jazz in France and in Europe generally. Its live appearances, however, were quite sparse at first. There was a limit to the number of concerts the Hot Club could put on, there were not yet any jazz clubs as such, and most nightclubs expected all-round music for dancing. That left the variety stage, but the band's first appearance as a supporting act at the Salle Pleyel ended in disaster. The singer Jean Tranchant, topping the bill, demanded that the Quintette should remain on-stage, in the dark, throughout his opening appearance, ready to launch into a number the moment the lights hit them. Tranchant's spot, which featured him bathed in lights of various colours, struck them as so ridiculous that they began to laugh. At first they managed to bottle it up, but finally Joseph Reinhardt exploded in a great, spluttering roar, which set the others off. That was the end of that engagement. The American impressario Irving Mills had come along that night especially to hear the Quintette. He walked out.

Another problem when it came to live performances was making sure that Django was present. He might be asleep, he might have met a friend and repaired for a game of billiards, he might have gone fishing. This was not absent-mindedness so much as the way he conducted his life. Django did not feel obliged to turn up for a job, because jobs were work, and work was what peasants did. Django did not work; he appeared. If the spirit did not move him to appear, he didn't appear.

For Grappelli, with all his anxieties and insecurities, life with Django could be torture at a practical level. On one occasion, when the Quintette was at the height of its success, it was honoured with an invitation to play for an after-dinner gathering at the Elysée Palace, the residence and office of the President of France. They presented themselves, correctly dressed, in good time – all except Django. After a death-defying drive in an official car through night-time Paris to Porte de Choisy, they found him in bed. Thrusting

Django was capable of great charm and exquisite politeness.

him into the the only clothes they could find in the caravan, they hustled him into the car. As the limousine drove in through the Palace gates, the guard saluted. "Ah!" murmured Django nodding graciously, "They recognise me!" He was wearing an ancient suit and a pair of slippers, and sporting two days' growth of beard, yet, even in these circumstances, he contrived to charm the company. Everyone who met Django was impressed by what has been described as his "princely bearing". Even the exasperated Grappelli was forced to admit that "his exquisite politeness was a lesson for everyone".

Django was very aware of the changing seasons. "He'd hear a bird and say, 'Oh, it's spring!'," Grappelli recalled. "Spring was my worst enemy, because when the leaves came on the trees, no Django!"

The Quintette's popularity grew steadily through 1935, and original compositions began to feature among its recordings. Two of these, Django's 'Blue Drag' and a Reinhardt-Grappelli collaboration, 'Ultrafox', date from the third session, in April. Like many of Django's most characteristic pieces, 'Blue Drag' is cast in a minor key. It is essentially a showpiece for Django himself, and there is a distinctly Gipsy, almost Spanish, flavour about it. 'Ultrafox', on the other hand, is a more conventionally 'jazzy' number, harmonically very close to the 1920s American song 'I'm Coming, Virginia'.

In March, Reinhardt and Grappelli both took part in a recording session by Coleman Hawkins, the world's leading tenor saxophonist at the time. They were there as members of Michel Warlop's orchestra. Stéphane, playing piano throughout, is heard only in the background, except for one four-bar introduction, but Django has two solos and his guitar is prominent in the rhythm section. Apart from Hawkins himself, the star of the show is the superb expatriate American trumpeter Arthur Briggs. Hawkins was already familiar with Django's playing, having sat in with him at several nightclubs. A year or so later, all American musicians visiting Paris would seek out Django Reinhardt, and that was largely because his name had been put about in the first place by Coleman Hawkins.

Overwhelming success

THROUGHOUT HIS EARLY CAREER, DJANGO played and recorded in all manner of contexts, especially as accompanist to French popular singers. Jean Sablon was the principal one, but there were also Éliane de Creus, Nane Cholet, Le Petit Mirsha and numerous others. As jazz grew in popularity and took up more and more of Django's attention, these gradually fell away. His last session with Sablon, in December 1935, was to all intents and purposes a Quintette session, but with Grappelli playing piano. Django is the soul of discretion throughout, but the casual elegance of his little obbligato phrases in 'Cette Chanson Est Pour Vous, Madame' and 'Rendezvous Sous La Pluie' completely steals the show.

Through its records, the Quintette du Hot Club de France became very popular with the growing jazz audience throughout Europe in the mid-1930s, although its live appearances continued to be sporadic. The personnel remained pretty stable, the only changes being in the rhythm guitar department. Joseph was there most of the time, but Chaput tended to come and go, his place being taken by one or other of Django's cousins, Eugene Vées and Pierre 'Baro' Ferret (or Ferré). Over the five years of its existence, there were no significant changes in the band's style. It had been developed in secret and presented to the public in a complete and polished state. You can pick out individual recordings by the Quintette at random and find all its qualities – invention, swing, melodic charm – on display.

To take just a few outstanding moments from 1936, the band's first year under its new recording contract with Pathé-Marconi: Django's solo on 'Limehouse Blues' is a tour de force, even for him. Structurally it is quite complex, alternating single-string phrases with passages in octaves and, in the second chorus, building to the sort of punchy, full-voiced statements employed by big bands of the period. But the main impression is of being carried along by the sheer impetus of the thing. The tempo is quite fast, and it feels even faster because of the urgency which Django generates. The same is true of 'After You've Gone', where he enters following Freddy Taylor's vocal chorus and hands over to Stéphane with a phrase in octaves that sets him off, swinging wildly. Django's theme statement at the start of 'Georgia On My Mind' is a delightful mixture of sentiment and mischievousness. The sentiment is already there in Hoagy Carmichael's tune, but the odd, spiky comments in between the phrases of the melody are pure, wayward Django.

The year 1937 was a particularly productive one for Django. In April, the Quintette recorded several sessions for Pathé-Marconi, and Django made his solo debut on record. The two pieces, 'Improvisation' and 'Parfum', have little or no stylistic connection with jazz, but they do show off his amazing technique. In the same month came the first recording by Europe's first specialist jazz record label, Swing Records. The band, specially assembled for the date, featured Coleman Hawkins on tenor saxophone, the American multi-instrumentalist Benny Carter, American drummer Tommy Benford, living in Paris at the time, saxophonists André Ekyan and Alix Combelle, bassist Eugène d'Hellemes, Stéphane (playing piano) and Django. The ensemble was given the name Coleman Hawkins and his All-Star Jam Band. For most of the time, Django plays rhythm guitar, although he has some brief solo moments on 'Honeysuckle Rose'. The four titles from this session have long been counted among the classic recordings of the swing era.

Over the summer of 1937, the Quintette was resident at the Big Apple, the establishment presided over by Bricktop, the 'Queen of Paris nightlife'. Born Ada Smith in Harlem in 1900, Bricktop possessed phenomenal social gifts. She could bring the most diverse people happily together, treat them all as friends and equals and make each one feel favoured to be in her presence. She accorded the musicians who played at her club the status of artists rather than employees, and this attitude communicated itself to the clientele. Django adored Bricktop, addressing her as 'Minou' ('Pussycat') and she was fond of him – to the extent of forgiving him for wearing brown shoes with evening dress. During the Quintette's residency, both Cole Porter and George Gershwin visited the club, Gershwin complimenting Grappelli on his rendition of 'Someone To Watch Over

LEFT **Multi-instrumentalist Benny Carter.** RIGHT **Coleman Hawkins spread Django's fame among visiting jazz players.**

Me'. The featured artist at the Big Apple was the British-born singer Mabel Mercer, revered by generations of other singers for her sensitive interpretation of American ballads. Grappelli accompanied her at the piano.

Americans flocked to Paris in the summer of 1937, despite the Depression, to attend the International Exposition taking place in the city. With them came a number of American entertainers, among them Eddie South, the 'Dark Angel of the Violin'. South was one of the few other violinists in jazz. His style was deeply imbued with the blues, and hence very different from Stéphane's. He often sat in at the Big Apple and recorded with both Django and Stéphane. His simple duet with Django, 'Eddie's Blues', shows not only what a compelling player he was, but how well Django adapted his style to fit in with him. Grappelli and South made a sparkling duet version of 'Daphne', accompanied by Django and the Quintette, a bravura 'Lady Be Good' with a 'trio de violons', completed by Michel Warlop, and an amazing 'swing improvisation' on the first movement of Bach's Double Violin Concerto, with Django standing in for the entire orchestra.

Also visiting Paris during the remarkable year of 1937 was the American big band led by Teddy Hill, in town to play for the 'Blackbirds' revue. Critic Hugues Panassié rounded up a select bunch of its members to make some records for the Swing label, among them trumpeters Bill Dillard and Shad Collins and trombonist Dicky Wells. Also in Hill's band was the 19-year-old Dizzy Gillespie, but he was considered too junior for the job and Bill Coleman, resident in Paris at the time, was called upon instead.

> Salvoes of applause crashed over their deserving heads

The results, which came out under Wells's name, were so good that they have scarcely been out of print since. Django's rhythm playing is a wonder of drive and variety. Behind one soloist he will confine himself to a sharp, clipped beat, then add a slight shuffle for the next, and so on. Since he is the only chordal rhythm instrument, everything he does can be heard very clearly. His solos, brief though they are, flow perfectly in and out of the ensemble. No wonder that, after the session, an impressed Dicky Wells remarked, "They don't come any better!"

Sales figures for the Quintette's records were particularly good in Britain, so it was only a matter of time before a British tour was proposed. It was to open with a gala London concert at the Cambridge Theatre on January 30th 1938. Anticipation was stoked up over several preceding weeks by the weekly musical paper *Melody Maker*, which was sponsoring the show, and all seats were quickly sold out. As expected, the concert was a triumph for the Quintette. At the end, the paper reported, "Salvoes of applause crashed over their deserving heads as they lined up in front of the tabs, grinning delightedly at their overwhelming success."

Equal praise went to Django and Stéphane. Critics referred to Django's "self-developed technique", "the subtle nuances imparted to every note" and the "terrific fecundity of his imagination". The *Melody Maker* report described Stéphane as "a polished, good-looking, grave-in-the-face sort of fellow who plays like an angel", singling

Bill Coleman stood in for Dizzy Gillespie.

out his "beautiful tone" and "facile technique". The succeeding tour of the provinces scored further success, and the whole trip confirmed the Quintette's fervent following in Britain, greater even than in France itself. This was partly due to the fact that, in Paris, its members took their own gigs and it was difficult to assemble them. Once abroad, they were obliged to stick together.

There were social reasons, too. In France, jazz was still overwhelmingly regarded as an adjunct to dining, dancing and nightlife in general, whereas in Britain, with its fast-growing subculture of dedicated swing fans, served by *Melody Maker* and other specialist press, it could be presented much more on its own terms. The same was true of Sweden, where the Quintette enjoyed a successful tour, early in 1939, billed as 'Reinhardt och Grappellys Franska Hotkvintett'.

While in London, the Quintette recorded for Decca. One of the pieces, co-composed by Stéphane and Django and played by them as a simple duet, is the haunting, impressionistic 'Nocturne'. It has a very similar quality to Bix Beiderbecke's piano pieces ('In A Mist', 'Candlelight', etc), neither jazz nor European salon music, but a subtle combination of the two. 'Nocturne' is perhaps the closest the pair of them ever came to expressing a perfectly unified sensibility. They were so different in almost everything, including many aspects of music, but here they are playing and feeling entirely as one.

The Quintette did manage to get together at home during 1938, notably for a recording session in May with the young virtuoso of the harmonica, Larry Adler, and for 'Une Nuit du Jazz' at Le Moulin de la Galette in Montmartre, scene of Renoir's famous painting of 1876, where they accompanied the American singer and trumpeter Valaida.

The outstanding event of spring 1939, from Django's point of view, was a recording session on April 5th with three members of Duke Ellington's orchestra, then touring in Europe: cornettist Rex Stewart, clarinettist Barney Bigard and bass player Billy Taylor. In his magisterial survey of the period, *The Swing Era*, the musicologist Gunther Schuller describes the five pieces recorded on that day as "all-time gems", to be counted "amongst the finest achievements of jazz". They are indeed very beautiful, with a quite different atmosphere from any other recordings in which Django ever took part.

Restrained, delicate and full of subtle tone-colours, they are jazz chamber music at its best, on a par with the recordings of the Kansas City Six or Billie Holiday with Teddy Wilson. Django plays one of his finest solos on 'Low Cotton', and the aptly-named 'Finesse' both begins and ends with his solo guitar. The records were credited to Rex Stewart's Big Four.

In August, the Quintette were back in London for another tour. Their new British agent, Lew Grade, had mentioned travels much further afield, as far as Australia and India. There was a further session for Decca. Among the numbers they recorded was a swing treatment of 'The Lambeth Walk', and for a couple of pieces they accompanied the young English singer Beryl Davis.

But it was an uneasy time. As the international situation deteriorated and war threatened, Britain prepared for the worst. Even the windows of the band's dressing room had been painted over, as part of the blackout preparations for impending bombing.

They had played two weeks of shows, finishing on Saturday September 2nd and were due to open at the State in Kilburn on Monday 4th. War was declared at 11am on Sunday 3rd, and soon after that the air-raid sirens were tested. Django immediately bolted for home, abandoning all his possessions, including his guitar. Grappelli stayed in London. Although

A picture of elegance: Grappelli and Reinhardt in 1939.

they were to meet and play together again after the war, this was effectively the end of their partnership.

It had never been an easy relationship, strained as it was by acute differences of background and temperament, but they owed more to one another than either would be prepared to admit. Had it not been for Django, Stéphane might never have liberated himself from the well-paid but unfulfilling life of an all-round jobbing musician. Without Stéphane's savoir faire, Django might never have become known beyond the bohemian circles of Paris. He certainly would never have learned to sign his own name, and finally

Django's autograph after Grappelli's coaching.

to write a few painful words in block capitals, because it was Grappelli who taught him.

Django was fully aware of his own lack of learning, and regarded Stéphane as the repository of all knowledge. He would suddenly come out with extraordinary questions, like "What's geography?" or "Where's Africa?" He remained particularly sensitive about his inability to read or write, although it caused him immense inconvenience. He couldn't travel on the Métro, for instance, because he was unable to read the names of the stations.

Most embarrassing of all, he couldn't sign his name on contracts. Stephane offered to teach him, and he agreed, so long as the lessons took place in complete privacy. He found 'Django' hard going, and settled simply for 'D', followed by 'Reinhardt'. Since letters meant nothing to him, he managed it by remembering the shape of the word and reproducing it.

"Once he had it, there was not enough paper in the room to satisfy him," Grappelli recalled. "Everywhere I looked I saw 'D Reinhardt'. It was a relief, because few things were ever more difficult than getting that man to sign his name. And it was worth the effort, because in his face I saw such pleasure."

Under the Nazis

BACK IN PARIS, DJANGO EXPLAINED why he had fled from London at the sound of the first air-raid siren. "You're less afraid at home," he said.

Nothing much happened at first, except that most foreigners left Paris, including Americans, although the US had not yet entered the war. One of the few who didn't go was a black American pianist named Charlie Lewis. He and Django put together a band of around 12 pieces, with a somewhat changeable personnel that included trumpeter Philippe Brun, saxophonists André Ekyan and Alix Combelle and various others, including the odd cousin. It was called Django's Music, and it appeared at Jimmy's Bar. The band recorded for Pathé at a marathon session on 22 February 1940. The best pieces are those in which the band acts purely as a frame for Django's guitar. The arrangements are slightly plodding, although efficiently played, but Django is not in the least put off and improvises with all the freedom and inventiveness of his days with Stéphane. He is particularly good in the Reinhardt-Grappelli piece, 'Tears', and a little riff tune called 'At The Jimmy's Bar'.

Musicians were being drafted into the French army, André Ekyan among them. As a replacement, a young man named Hubert Rostaing presented himself. He had been recommended by Alix Combelle, although he was very unsure of himself. He liked jazz, but didn't think he could really play it. His audition consisted of sitting in a bar with Django, drinking Armagnac. When he turned up at Jimmy's, his performance on the tenor saxophone was woeful and he picked up his clarinet in the hope that his inexperience would be less obvious. Django stopped playing, looked over at him and said, "You want to stick with that. It sounds good." From that moment Rostaing became a clarinet player, and later an important part of Django's musical life.

The war was on, men were being drafted, but life in Paris went on more or less as before. Feeling safe behind its impregnable Maginot Line, France waited for everything to return to normal. And then the unthinkable happened. The Germans bypassed the Line, overran Belgium, Luxembourg and northern France and, on June 14th 1940, entered Paris. There was panic. Convinced that the city was about to be razed to the ground, thousands, Django and Naguine among them, fled south, blocking the roads and causing chaos. After an armistice had been signed and civil order restored, Parisians gradually drifted back to the occupied city.

America was still officially neutral, but the German authorities condemned American culture as decadent and banned the showing of American films. This set off an extraordinary public reaction in France, especially among the young. It took the form of "If the Boche are against, we're all for it", and almost instantly a whole new youth culture arose, based on things American. Films might be banned, but there was always music. American musicians might have departed, but France had its own jazz musicians. Many of these acquired star status almost overnight. Django Reinhardt was already one of the best-known, and he became a superstar.

His fame rested, of course, on the Hot Club Quintette which he now set about reviving. "I'm not going to pack it in just because Grappelli's not around," he told his friend Pierre Fouad. "Before the Germans came I heard a young guy who plays the clarinet pretty well. He's got a nice soft sound, plenty of drive, doesn't mind working. I've a good mind to take him on." And so the second Quintette du Hot Club de France was born, with a somewhat apprehensive Hubert Rostaing standing in Stéphane Grappelli's shoes.

We have it from Rostaing's own account that he practised like mad in the first few months. He certainly sounds on top of the job in the first recordings by the new Quintette, especially the slippery 'Rhythme Future'. The band is very different in sound from the original Quintette, not only because clarinet has replaced violin, but because there is now a drummer, and only one rhythm guitar. It some respects it is a more conventional sound, but the absence of Grappelli meant that Django was now the undoubted leader and had more freedom to experiment. For one session, towards the end of 1940, he brought in Alix Combelle to play clarinet alongside Rostaing and the effect is quite magical at times. The two clarinets fill out the melodic line without adding undue weight, and when they play short, stabbing riffs they sound uncannily like a double-stopped violin.

The question inevitably arises of how Django was able to carry on in the public eye like this. Were Gipsies not lumped together with Jews as racially inferior? Were they not persecuted and sent to concentration camps? This certainly was the policy. Of the estimated five million Gipsies in Europe before the war, half a million died in the camps. It is possible that disaster would eventually have overtaken Django, but it never did. His very popularity protected him to a large extent, and it was in the interests of the occupying forces to keep the French public as quiescent as possible. For the time being, so long as they didn't provoke the authorities too seriously, or indulge in acts of open defiance, people were left to get on with what had become a pretty miserable life.

At the forefront of the sudden craze for swing were a section of Parisian youth who called themselves 'Zazous'. They took the business of adopting decadent American ways with almost religious fervour. As far as shortages allowed, they aped Harlem fashions, combed their hair in elaborate styles, danced 'le jitterbug' as they remembered it from pre-war movies, and generally caused pain and outrage to their elders. It wasn't so much the Germans who felt pained by the Zazous as older, conservative French people. There was a widespread feeling among them that Germany was bound to win the war, and if France behaved itself and went along with the German occupation, things would eventually get better. We know now that they would prove to be mistaken, but they were timid people living through a frightening situation.

> They adopted decadent American ways with almost religious fervour

The Zazous were a small and extreme indication of a very large phenomenon. People who had never taken much notice of jazz (or 'swing' as it now came to be called) before the war certainly went for it in a big way after 1940. The popular craze for swing threw up all kinds of strange phenomena. Revues with titles like 'Le Swing de l'Amour' and 'Femmes et Rhythmes' drew large audiences, and there were queues outside cinemas showing the movie *Mademoiselle Swing*.

The trick was to play down the American connection. This was a difficult feat to bring off, but people like Delaunay made a few quite elegant moves. In one article he claimed that America had forfeited the right to be called the home of jazz. The music of Armstrong and Ellington, he wrote, was ignored and dishonoured in the country of its birth, being supplanted by cheap and flashy imitations. The Hot Club de France had two aims: to encourage appreciation of true jazz and promote the development of a distinctive *jazz français*.

Another, slightly less tortuous ploy was to replace the titles of well-known American tunes with French translations. Django's recorded output from the years of occupation is full of delightful examples: 'Indecision' ('Undecided'), 'Petits Mensonges' ('Little White Lies'), 'Sur les Bords de l'Alamo' ('On The Alamo'), 'De Nul Part' ('Out Of Nowhere'), and so on. He was, of course, careful to give his own tunes French titles.

Those composed during this period include two of his most beautiful melodies, 'Nuages' and 'Manoir de Mes Rêves'.

Django's period of superstardom continued through 1941 and beyond. His picture was to be seen on posters all over Paris, and on postcards for sale in tabacs. Tales of his free-and-easy Gipsy life in his caravan went the rounds, although in fact he was now ensconced in a luxury flat on the Champs-Elysées. One such story concerned Django taking a break during a gig, eating a baked hedgehog that one of his cousins had brought along for him. A patron watched him in horrified fascination.

"What's that? It looks like a rat!"

"Oh yes, it's a rat all right," replied Django, winking at his cousin. "Very tasty, too."

Fame brought its rewards but also its little annoyances, such as accusations of being an impostor. It happened when he was appearing at Le Doyen. An irate character called for the head waiter and demanded to be taken to confront "this so-called Django Reinhardt". He had just returned, he said, from six months in a prisoner-of-war camp where he had lived in the same hut as Django Reinhardt. "This fellow looks a bit like him, but you can't fool me. I should know, I slept in the next bed to the real one for six months!" Another of the cousins, no doubt.

The constant shortages and the restrictions on daily life had a wearing, claustrophobic effect on everyone. Travel was difficult, but Django managed to get the Quintette away from Paris for tours. In the spring of 1942 they visited Belgium and in the summer they headed for the Riviera. These trips made a great deal of money. "He came back with gold watches on each wrist," Rostaing recalled. "His wife had bracelets all over her arms, round her ankles, anywhere there was room for them. Anything that remained he gambled away." The problem was that when Django had plenty of money he became unbearable, according to Rostaing. He didn't feel like working and only turned up to play with a bad grace. After Nice, the Quintette embarked for Algiers, where it was to play at a theatre. When he learned that he was expected to play two shows a day, Django simply caught the next boat home, leaving the rest of the band behind. They managed to get out just before the Allied forces landed in North Africa.

When Django turned down his request for a rise, bearing in mind all the money the Quintette had made, Rostaing left the band. His place was taken first by André Lluis and later by Gérard Lévêque. The two alternated for a while, sometimes teaming up to revive the two-clarinet version of the Quintette.

Although he rebelled against the routine of regular appearances and, according to Rostaing, often sounded bored and desultory during long tours, Django made some phenomenal records with the Lévêque-Lluis Quintette during 1942-3. The two-clarinet version of 'Manoir de Mes Rêves' is quite outstanding, with the guitar floating above the melody, played in serene unison by the clarinets. There is also an amazing 'Django Rag', a marvel of technique, taken at the fastest tempo he ever recorded, and superb performances of some of his most attractive compositions, including 'Belleville', 'Douce Ambience', 'Fleur d'Ennui' and 'Blues d'Autrefois'.

Composition was very much on Django's mind at this period. He confided to

In the war years, Django joined France's pantheon of stars, along with singer Edith Piaf

Lévêque that he had been hatching ideas for larger musical works, including a symphony based on the theme of 'Manoir de Mes Rêves'. He had recorded a few pieces with big bands, but they had been professionally arranged purely as accompaniments for his guitar. He was after something more personal, something he could hear in his head but lacked the ability to get down on paper. Lévêque offered to help, and even moved in temporarily to Django's flat.

"Every night, once we got back," he told Charles Delaunay, "Django would lie down and spend the rest of the night playing. We'd stop to eat and drink, but that was all. He'd play each instrument's part on his guitar and I'd get it down on paper. It was there we began to get down the famous symphony, 'Manoir de Mes Rêves'."

So certain was Django that this was to be his debut as a serious composer that he had a hall and orchestra booked and the concert advertised. But when the conductor, Jo Bouillon, first glanced at the score he declared that it was too harmonically daring and strange – 'too modern', in short – and refused to take it on. And that wasn't the only difficulty. There was to have been a choir, but the choral parts had not been written. Jean Cocteau had promised to write the words the choir would sing, but he had not been given a synopsis. Through it all, Lévêque himself had grave misgivings about his own competence in handling such a big task. So the concert never took place. The score was passed around in the hope of finding someone willing to take it on, and was eventually lost.

There remained a few pieces for conventional big band that Django and Lévêque had worked on, including 'Belleville' and 'Oubli'. Django recorded these with Fud Candrix's band, and performed them at a Paris concert, although even that almost failed happen. Django had not turned

> Django concluded that the time had come to make himself scarce

up when he was due to appear. Lévêque rushed to his flat and found him asleep. Dragging Django down to the street, he hailed a passing motorcyclist. Django, still half asleep, arrived at the stage door riding on the pillion.

The German authorities now began suggesting that Django might care to play a few shows in the Fatherland, to help demonstrate how happy the French nation was to be part of the Greater Reich. The suggestions gradually grew more frequent and more insistent, until Django concluded that the time had come to make himself scarce. He and Naguine would take a holiday at Thonon-les-Bains, near the Swiss border, and, when the chance arose, get across into neutral Switzerland. But it is hard to disappear when you are a superstar. No sooner had they arrived on the peaceful shores of Lac Leman than they ran into a band of Gipsies, who recognised Django instantly. Food, drink and guitars were produced, with the inevitable consequences. Soon the entire population of Thonon-les-Bains knew that the great Django had arrived in their midst. A local café turned itself into a little club, Lévêque and Jourdon, the drummer, arrived from Paris and for the following month it was business as usual.

Finally, the escape attempt was set up. Django and Naguine made their way to an obscure café to meet their guide, only to find it full of German soldiers. The couple looked so nervous that they were arrested on suspicion of spying and escorted to the guardhouse. There they made Django turn out his pockets, where they found his membership card of the British Performing Rights Society, the body that collects royalties on behalf of composers. Django was a member only because the equivalent French organisation refused to accept him, on the grounds that he could neither read nor write music.

It seemed as though the PRS card would prove his undoing. Then occurred one of those impossible strokes of luck which befall all gamblers once or twice in their lives. Django was marched off to be interrogated by the unit's commander. The officer glanced up from his paperwork, took one look at the prisoner and cried, "Reinhardt? Good God, man! What are you doing here?" Django had run into a jazz fan. After apologising for causing so much trouble, promising not to do it again and, no doubt, signing his 'D Reinhardt' autograph, he was escorted from the premises.

Now it was the turn of the French to be suspicious. They had seen him being taken into the guardhouse, and seen him leave half an hour later, with smiles and handshakes all round. This could only mean one thing – the man was a collaborator. Nobody would speak to him or have anything to do with him or Naguine. It was unbearable. Only one thing for it. If he went alone he might be able to get across, and arrange for Naguine to be brought over later. That night he set off, crossing no-man's land without mishap and crawling under the barbed wire. As he emerged into Switzerland, he found himself staring at a pair of polished boots. The Swiss guards interrogated him on the spot. Was he an escaped prisoner of war? No. Was he a Jew? No. Then he couldn't come in. The rules were quite clear. He'd have to go back again. They gave him something to eat and took him to a spot where it was possible to climb over the barbed wire, back into occupied Europe. Once across, he called at a farmhouse to clean himself up, made his way back to Thonon-les-Bains, picked up Naguine and headed for Paris.

The fruits of liberty

THE FACT THAT DJANGO WAS SAVED by the intervention of a jazz-loving German officer may seem far-fetched, but jazz lovers were by no means unknown in the ranks of the Wehrmacht. People do not change all that much when they are drafted, and the gulf between the official Nazi line in cultural matters and soldiers' private tastes could be enormous. In his fascinating book *La Tristesse de Saint Louis* (subtitled 'Swing Under the Nazis'), Mike Zwerin recounts the stories of many jazz lovers in German uniform indulging their passion for the music.

Perhaps the most remarkable of these was Oberleutnant Dietrich Schulz-Köhn of the Luftwaffe. He had met Django during a pre-war visit to Paris, and had actually become a member of the Hot Club de France. Once in the armed forces, he not only circulated an underground jazz newsletter, but, while stationed in Paris, had himself photographed in the street outside La Cigale, alongside Django and five other musicians. After the war he would show the picture round delightedly with the words, "Here I am in full uniform, with a Gipsy, four Negroes and a Jew!" In the dying days of the war, while negotiating with an American unit near St Nazaire under a flag of truce, Schultz-Köhn asked politely, "I wonder, do you have any Count Basie records?"

Back in Paris, Django collected the Quintette together and they set off on another tour. Once again, the regularity of the whole business soon began to irk him and he grew fretful. In Monte Carlo he put down his guitar and walked off the stage because the audience was "too noisy". In Bayonne he refused to appear because he had no clean shirt to wear. The band travelled by train, and the trains were always crowded because of wartime disruption. Allied air attacks on German installations in France were intensifying, with the result that they were constantly having to dive into shelters. Everyone was glad to get back to Paris, although there were air-raids there, too.

The Quintette opened at a small club in Rue Pigalle, appropriately called La Roulotte ('The Caravan'), which the owner renamed Chez Django Reinhardt in his honour. The only problem was that it was too small for the crowds who wanted to get in, and when it was full there was no room for the band. Nevertheless, Django played the part of 'patron' to perfection. Naguine was pregnant and the couple were living in a nearby house that had been abandoned and was in a very bad state. Although it was spring, the weather was cold and Django chopped up the furniture to feed the fire. It was here that their son, Babik, was born, on June 8th, two days after D-Day, the start of the Allied invasion of Europe.

Paris was liberated on August 25th 1944. The war was by no means over, and life remained hard, but the atmosphere changed immediately and totally. US troops were encamped on the Avenue de la Grande Armée, Jeeps roared around the streets and 'degenerate' American culture was back on the menu in a big way. During the course of the war, both sides had exploited the power of entertainment, especially popular music, but the United States had made it a major part of its propaganda effort. The best-known figure in this campaign was Captain (later Major) Glenn Miller and his Army Air Force orchestra, which had been broadcasting from London since June 1944, to both Allied troops and the enemy. These latter shows were presented in German, with the lyrics of current US song hits specially translated for the purpose. But Miller's was by no means the only one. Virtually every branch of the US armed forces had its full-time band, and Britain also contributed its share. As well as live entertainment, the US forces were served by their own radio network, the Armed Forces Radio Service, and their own record label, V-Disc. One of the very first installations to be set up on European soil following the invasion was a radio transmitter.

In those first few months of freedom, American stars who had become icons in occupied Paris might materialise anywhere. In September, the Quintette were in the wings of the Olympia theatre, waiting to go on, when an American officer strode over to Django and clapped him on the shoulder, saying, "I remember you! I heard you at the London Palladium in 1938! Wonderful!" It was Fred Astaire.

Glenn Miller died on December 15th 1944, when his aircraft disappeared over the Channel in bad weather. He had been on his way to organise the transfer of his orchestra's headquarters from England to France. The move went ahead, with the band now under the leadership of drummer Ray McKinley. Just as in the old days, once they had settled in, the musicians set out in search of the famous Django. They found him playing with the Quintette at Le Tabarin. Soon, pianist Mel Powell, saxophonist Peanuts Hucko, trumpeter Bernie Privin and other members of the Miller band were sitting in regularly at the club. According to Gérard Lévêque, "Sometimes our band looked as though it was made up completely of American servicemen." Django and the Miller men recorded four numbers together in a Paris studio on 25th January, although Army regulations officially forbade service musicians to take outside engagements. Since Ray McKinley, their leader, played drums on the session they can't have taken the rule too seriously, although the records did first come out under the name of 'Jazz Club Mystery Hot Band'. They are pleasant, relaxed performances, with Powell, Privin and Django showing up as the most impressive soloists.

Django's presence acted as a magnet to guitar players in particular. A report in *Down Beat* magazine, by Lieutenant Herb Caen, dated 1st March 1945, says: "As you might imagine, Django's spot is the gathering place for every guitarist in Paris. In fact, the night we dropped in, there were more string-pluckers in the house than you'd find at an Andre (sic) Segovia concert."

Fred Astaire sought out Django in liberated Paris.

A more formal alliance was made with the the band of US Air Transport Command (ATC). Django appeared as guest star with them at concerts and in broadcasts over AFN, the American Forces Network, towards the end of 1945. Django always relished the experience of being star of the show, apparently in command of a big, powerful orchestra. In fact, the orchestra usually adjusted its customary arrangements to make room for Django's solos, but the recordings made by AFN at the time show that the setup worked pretty well. They are especially valuable because they include two of the orchestrations which Lévêque had written for Django to perform with the Belgian band of Fud Candrix during the war – 'Djangology' and 'Belleville'. Army regulations must have been relaxed by now, because the entire ATC orchestra temporarily became Django Reinhardt & his American Swing Band at a session for the Swing label in November. This produced a repeat performance of 'Djangology', a slightly rushed 'Swing Guitars' and yet another version of 'Manoir de Mes Rêves', in which the arranger, Lonnie Wolfgong, tried out a few mildly Ellingtonian effects.

Meanwhile, Stéphane Grappelli had spent the war in England. It had not taken him long to become established, first as a member of the resident band at Hatchett's Club and later as a musical attraction in his own right – "The world's greatest swing violinist." By 1945 he had a successful career, a first-class agent in Lew Grade, a circle of devoted friends, a London flat overlooking Green Park and a country cottage in Devon (complete with housekeeper). He had also found a new musical partner, a young, blind pianist from Battersea named George Shearing, who shared the solo limelight in his British sextet. To complete his good fortune, the delicate health which had dogged him for most of his life appeared to have been cured by a timely kidney operation.

The two former partners had each had a 'good war'. In France, Django had achieved stardom almost in the Maurice Chevalier league, while Stéphane had found more modest fame in England, but also a contentment he had never known before. The question now was, could they pick up where they had left off, or had they both changed too much? Stéphane was now leading the band at Hatchett's, so it was agreed to hold the reunion in London and that Charles Delaunay would accompany Django, Naguine and the infant Babik.

As described by Delaunay, it was an emotional meeting: "There they were. They couldn't say a word. Then Stéphane opened his case, took out his violin and began to play 'La Marseillaise', and Django immediately joined in. They couldn't speak … After that, there were embraces, cries of 'Mon frère!' and a jam session until dawn."

The reunion took place on January 26th 1946. A few days later a temporary Hot Club Quintette was assembled in London, consisting of two British guitarists, Jack Llewellyn and Allan Hodgkiss, the great Jamaican bassist, Coleridge Goode, Stéphane and Django. This group recorded two sessions for Decca during that week. If anything, the result sounds better-integrated than the original band. This is partly because Coleridge Goode is an infinitely better player than Louis Vola, but the two soloists play with marvellous fluency and sound totally at ease. 'Coquette' and 'Django's Tiger' ('Tiger Rag') are particularly fine examples. The programme also includes a recreation of the 'Marseillaise' moment, which did not meet with official approval back home, even though the recording was given the title 'Echoes Of France'.

Plans had been made for a British tour and a series of broadcasts on BBC radio, but Django was suddenly smitten by a mysterious illness and rushed to the French hospital in London. After making a slow recovery, with all the projected plans cancelled, he returned to Paris. He had not been expected back and there was little for him to do, apart from a recording session for Pathé, in May, with Hubert Rostaing. He took up painting to pass the time. It was an activity that occupied him, on and off, for the rest of his life.

Ever since his childhood, Django had been fascinated by the idea of America. Before the war, one of his favourite pastimes had been going to the cinema to see American films. America was the home of jazz, and he was a jazz star. In his mind's eye he saw himself as a kind of Clark Gable figure, romantic and irresistible. Quite often he would tell people that he would be leaving for the US within a week or so, although no such plans had been made. The war, by making his American dream unattainable, only served to intensify its appeal. Now, in October 1946, came the offer of a US tour, as guest-star with Duke Ellington's orchestra.

He arrived in New York without a guitar, convinced that Gibson, Gretsch, Martin and every other guitar manufacturer in the United States would be lining up at the dockside, pressing instruments on him. But they were not, and one had to be bought for him. He joined the Ellington band in Cleveland, in time for a brief rehearsal before the first

Django and Stéphane, reunited in London in 1946, with Coleridge Goode (bass) and two British guitarists, Allan Hodgkiss and Jack Llewellyn (obscured).

concert. Since Django spoke no English and no-one else could speak much French, the proceedings were brief.

They settled on a simple formula, as Ellington later explained: "We would just hit him with a pin spot and he'd be sitting there, black out the whole stage, he'd state some theme, every night it was a different theme, and none of this stuff was recorded ... He'd play those wonderful things and just sit there in that one soft spot and play and play. So much happening there. It was a gas!"

The orchestra travelled by train, in its own special coaches. Despite the lack of a common language, Django got on famously with Ellington and the other musicians. The one thing he couldn't get over was their spectacular, floral-patterned underwear. The tour made its way to Chicago, then on through Detroit, Pittsburg, St Louis, Kansas City and other cites. Django proved very popular with audiences and all went smoothly until they reached New York. This was to be the climax of the tour, with two concerts at Carnegie Hall. The first of these went very well, with Django taking six curtain calls.

On the second night, however, he failed to appear until the show was nearly over. In the street, that afternoon, he had run into the French boxer Marcel Cerdan and they had passed some pleasant hours together, talking over old times. Suddenly realising how late it was, Django hailed a cab and asked to be taken to Carnegie Hall. The driver, however, misunderstood and drove him to a remote spot in the suburbs. He finally arrived backstage at 11pm, and managed to squeeze in a couple of numbers before the close. The critics were not impressed.

The hoped-for US career failed to materialise. He played a month with clarinettist Edmond Hall's band at Café Society in Greenwich Village and, when nothing else turned up, left for home. Apart from the experience of playing with Ellington, the only bright spot of the whole adventure had been visiting Madison Square Garden, in company with Jean Sablon, where they watched Cerdan beat Adams, the American challenger.

"When I asked him later for his impressions of America," wrote Charles Delaunay in his memoir of Django, "he seemed to me to have lost all his illusions. He was far from impressed by the American mentality, above all that of the women. Even the cars no longer had their old appeal for him; they were all too much alike." Apart from the Carnegie Hall debacle, the main cause of his disillusion was probably loneliness. A gregarious and hospitable man, he was lost in a country where no-one spoke his language and whose ways he found cold and alien. He was homesick and desperately missed his wife and little son.

Tastes change

Django with Duke Ellington in Chicago during their 1946 concert tour.

DJANGO ARRIVED HOME ON FEBRUARY 13TH 1947 in a dejected mood. The American tour had not been an total disaster, but neither had it been a triumph. Concert audiences had been generally enthusiastic, but the Café Society crowd had not shown any great excitement. To the American jazz world at large he was a passing curiosity, and to the music business he was the guy who turned up late at

Carnegie Hall. By the time he sailed for home most American fans had already forgotten all about him.

He opened at Le Boeuf sur le Toit three weeks later, leading an 11-piece band, later slimmed-down to six. Soon after the opening, Stéphane Grappelli turned up on a short visit and received a tumultuous reception when he sat in at the club. Still nothing had been said about reconstituting the Quintette under the original partnership. Neither of them seemed in a hurry to enter into such a commitment. Indeed, once the euphoria of their reunion had passed, they treated each other with a certain distance, all amiability on the surface but a lot of caution underneath. Nevertheless, they got together on March 26th to record four numbers for Pathé, with Joseph Reinhardt and Jean Ferret on guitars and Emmanuel Soudieux on bass. Superficially, these sound like a simple continuation of the Quintette tradition, but there are hints of something else. It shows itself in the occasional angularity of phrase, or a line that ends in a strange, unfinished way – for example the seventh and eighth bars of Django's new, oddly titled number 'R-Vingt Six'. This new element was bebop.

Isolated by the war from new developments in jazz, Europe found this complex new jazz style, hatched during the early 1940s by Charlie Parker, Dizzy Gillespie and others, utterly bewildering at first. To some it was a rich and fascinating musical language and they couldn't get enough of it. To others it was just weird, nervous and cold, nothing like the warm, joyous, wholehearted music that they had grown to love. But for a while, in the late 1940s, bebop was fashionable and its phraseology invaded many areas of popular music. Even Frank Sinatra recorded a novelty song entitled 'Bop Goes My Heart' in 1948. It is hardly surprising, therefore, that the Quintette's work at this period should echo this new style, if only faintly. It would, in any case, have been impossible to play full-blown bebop using the Quintette line-up, with its heavy four-in-a-bar rhythm guitar and a bass as often as not playing two-to-the-bar.

Nevertheless, Django was clearly fascinated by the new approach. Pierre Michelot, who played bass with him in later years, maintained that it was the sheer audacity of bebop that captivated him, and from 1947 onwards his style clearly veered in that direction. In April of that year he recorded a new tune, 'Pêche à la Mouche' ('Fly-Fishing', one of his favourite pastimes), with a quintet that was pointedly billed as Django Reinhardt et son Quintette, no mention of the Hot Club. It consisted of Michel de Villers on alto saxophone, pianist Eddie Bernard, bassist Willy Lockwood, Al Craig on drums – and Joseph playing rhythm guitar, which sticks out like a sore thumb. The tune is a spiky little riff, not quite bebop but on the verge. The whole performance gives the impression of pulling in two directions at once, with Django and deVillers tending towards bebop and the rhythm section steered firmly down the established path by Joseph. It is exactly the kind of thing one encounters in early Charlie Parker recordings from the war years, when he found himself teamed with players of a previous generation.

It is possible that, given a totally free hand, Django might have made a clean break with the past and got himself a whole new band, but he was not in that position. Setting aside questions of obligation to his brother and the numerous cousins who passed through the Quintette's rhythm guitar ranks, plus the problem of finding competent bebop players in post-war France, there was the necessity of providing what entertainers' contracts call "the Act as known". The name of Django Reinhardt immediately suggested to the public the chugging rhythm of the Quintette's two rhythm guitars, and they would not buy anything else.

Add to this the fact that times were getting hard. Genuine American glamour was now available and local stars, even superstars, were feeling the pinch. French film makers and actors led a protest march in Paris against the flood of American movies that threatened to sweep away their industry. Jazz musicians, as is their wont, grumbled endlessly in bars about declining work opportunities.

The problem for Django and his generation was compounded by the fact that jazz itself was rent in two by an ideological conflict. The bebop revolution had ignited a counter-revolution, in the form of the traditional jazz movement. This championed the early jazz of New Orleans and Chicago, claiming this to be the only real, authentic form of the music. The dispute was a world-wide phenomenon, but the French, with their tradition of fierce intellectual engagement, fell upon it with relish. Concert promoters soon learned not to mix modern and traditional bands on the same bill, as one lot of partisan supporters booed and whistled at the band favoured by the other lot, and vice versa. When Dizzy Gillespie brought his big band to Paris in 1948, the modernists were ecstatic. When the veteran Sidney Bechet of New Orleans arrived the following year, the traditionalists treated him like the Pope.

And what of those jazz musicians who were neither beboppers nor traditionalists? They were simply ignored. When the first Nice Jazz Festival was held, in February 1948, both wings were lavishly represented (on separate stages, naturally) but the Quintette du Hot Club de France was at first left out. It was only when the Mayor, who was sponsoring the event, banged the table and demanded it that the band was included at all.

Django and Stéphane had agreed, in November 1947, to revive the Quintette in its original form. It was relaunched with a concert at the Salle Pleyel, followed by four weeks at the ABC Music Hall. The Pleyel concert was sold out, but attendances after that were not encouraging. Critics all said the same thing: both Reinhardt and Grappelli played beautifully, but they failed to spark each other off as in the old days. Recordings made at around the time of the Nice Festival bear this out. There are some superb individual performances, particularly in 'Festival 48', a boppish little piece composed by Django specially for the Nice appearance, but the ensembles are efficient rather than exciting.

The band was then booked for a tour of England, where it had always had a keen and loyal following. When the five arrived in London they found that their luggage had been stolen. Joseph Reinhardt, Challin Ferret and the bassist Emmanuel Soudieux interpreted this as an ill omen and went straight back to Paris. Stéphane and Django carried on with British replacements and kept them on for a month-long tour of Scandinavia. They returned to Paris after that, but there were no further plans for the Reinhardt-Grappelli version of the Quintette. To all intents and purposes this marked end of their partnership, except for a two-month tour in Italy, early in 1949, where the

Together again: Reinhardt and Grappelli in 1949

two of them were accompanied by local musicians. It was in Rome, during January and February, that they made their final recordings together.

In all, they recorded 62 tracks. Not all of them saw the light of day, but those that were issued make fascinating, sometimes bizarre listening. Stéphane plays with expansive grace for the most part, sounding better than ever for much of the time. Django, on the other hand, seems to be in a state of creative agitation. A typical example comes in their version of Charles Trenet's sentimental ballad, 'La Mer'. Stéphane was a master at this kind of tune, giving it the full romantic treatment but never quite slipping over into mawkishness. While he is doing this, Django, behind him, is clearly following a totally different script, interpolating loud bebop licks and thunderous tremolos. It is rather like listening to a man reading out a passionate love-letter while, in the same room, Laurel and Hardy are busy smashing up the furniture.

Nevertheless, there are some nice moments in these Italian records, including a tune named after 'Bricktop', in which Stéphane plays the theme pizzicato in unison with Django, a version of 'What Is This Thing Called Love?' which incorporates the Parker-Gillespie theme 'Hot House', and Django's riff tune 'Artillerie Lourde' ('Heavy Artillery'), aptly named in the circumstances. Just occasionally, there are flashes of the old close partnership, for instance in 'Marie', which swings with glorious freedom.

Once the Italian tour was over, they parted and never formally played together again. It has often been said that Stéphane Grappelli only really came into his own when he had escaped from the shadow of Django Reinhardt. Certainly, his playing grew and deepened with the years and, although Django had been a source of inspiration to him, he had also been the cause of endless trouble, anxiety and embarrassment. In public, he generally spoke warmly of his old partner, but sometimes he would reflect that his life would have been easier without him. "Ah! What troubles he gave me!" he told an interviewer towards the end of his life. "I think now I would rather play with lesser musicians and have a peaceable time than with Django and his monkey business." Stéphane outlived Django by 44 years, slightly longer that Django's entire life-span.

Back in Paris, as the 1940s drew to a close, Django found the jazz scene so changed that he felt he didn't fit in any more. His reaction was to damn the lot of them and take to the road. He bought an ancient Lincoln Zephyr, hooked it up to a new caravan and, with Naguine and Babik aboard, set off. They got no further than the suburb of Le Bourget before the Lincoln broke down. Fortunately, there was a Manouche community close by, and that is where they settled for a while.

The question now arises, how did he manage to support himself and his family, especially since he spent or gambled away any cash he happened to get? The answer is that, apart from a mysterious ability to acquire food, drink, tobacco, etc, apparently without money changing hands, he had an income from royalties on his compositions. His work was published by the British firm of Francis Day, and his royalties collected by the Performing Right Society of Great Britain. PRS, whose membership card had landed him in deadly danger during the war, was and is a meticulous body. Django composed a huge number of tunes, and every time he recorded a new one it was logged. These royalties, inaccessible to him during the war, had built up a sizeable backlog, to which were now added the pieces composed while the war had been in progress. And because the money came in regular, moderate amounts, he couldn't spend it all at once. Quite by accident, he had provided himself with the spendthrift gambler's perfect financial support system.

The long-suffering André Ekyan finally ran Django to earth at Le Bourget and asked where he was working. "Nowhere," replied Django. His excuse was that half of his front teeth had fallen out, so he couldn't appear on stage, and he was scared of dentists. Ekyan finally got him into a dentist's chair, where a further six teeth had to be removed. Once he had been fitted with a set of dentures he felt better about picking up the guitar again. This time he finally broke away from the Hot Club format, although he hung on to the name for a while. His bands from now on would have the modern piano-bass-drums rhythm section, usually with himself and a saxophone or clarinet in front – and he would be playing amplified guitar. He had experimented with amplification from time to time, although never seriously, but the electric guitar was now a serious solo instrument in jazz and he was determined to adopt it.

Electric to the end

EKYAN SET OUT CONFIDENTLY to organise a season of engagements for himself and the revitalised, electrified Django, but found the job harder than he'd imagined. There were a couple of weeks at a smart Paris restaurant, where the new band failed to impress, then a brief residency at Le Touquet, followed by a sparse tour in France. The spring of 1950 found Django back in Italy, and in the same studio where he had recorded with Grappelli the previous year.

It must be said that the new band, still billed as the Quintette du Hot Club de France, sounds pretty lacklustre. Ekyan plays alto saxophone much of the time, and he is simply

Django was never more at home than with his Gipsy family and friends.

not an incisive enough player to share the lead with Django. The rhythm section, too, has that insipid, sedate air about it which anyone who remembers the 1950s will associate with hotel dance bands. Most of the 30 numbers follow the pattern of theme – string of solos – theme, which is fine if all the soloists are equally strong, but here it is a matter of a chorus of Django sandwiched between nondescript choruses from Ekyan and pianist Ralph Schécroun. The electric guitar still sounds like Django, but its tone lacks the texture of the acoustic. Django has obviously been listening to Charlie Christian, or some of his many disciples, because his improvised lines are more even and flowing. It is noticeable, too, that he has abandoned the furniture-smashing act, probably because, whereas Stéphane could sail blithely through it all, Ekyan and the others would have been completely sunk.

It was all very unsatisfactory and depressing, and far too much like working and living the life of a peasant. As soon as the Italian trip was finished, Django abandoned all idea of hanging on to the revised Quintette. He dropped the whole thing, returned to Le Bourget and spent his time fishing, painting, playing billiards and generally pleasing himself. Occasionally someone would come up with an offer, but only rarely was he tempted to go out and play. One approach that did mildly interest him was to appear as guest soloist on a Radio Luxembourg broadcast with Jaques Helian's big band. As long as Gérard Lévêque would come and work out the arrangements with him, he would do it. Lévêque duly reported to the encampment at Le Bourget.

"His mother was living in an old Citroën that had been fitted out as a van," Lévêque recalled, "and beside it was Django's caravan, a real beauty. We found Django in a large shed nearby, where he was busy building a new caravan … We chattered about everything under the sun except the scores, and the broadcast was due to take place that very afternoon! Meanwhile, Django had taken a fat roll of banknotes out from beneath his pillow. He gave his wife one or two of them so that she could go and get a chicken and some bottles of wine … Finally, Django took down his guitar. It was ages since he'd played it. It was covered with dust and the strings were dull and rusty. I just had time to note down the chief melodic lines of 'Double Whisky' that he played me. It was a good job I was used to working with him."

Amazingly, Lévêque finished the arrangement and the broadcast took place as planned. That was in July 1950. Nothing more was seen or heard of Django for the rest of that year. It was assumed that he had lost interest in music and given it up as a bad job. In fact, he had only lost interest in the boring incidentals of music – the touring schedules, the nightclubs with their diners and dancers, the hanging about backstage in theatres. But the Paris jazz scene had changed once more. With the dawn of the 1950s began the great era of the bohemian Left Bank, with its smoky dives frequented by students, artists and intellectuals. Prominent among these was Club Saint-Germain in Rue St. Benoît, where the atmosphere was informal but attentive, and where all an artist was required to do was play his best. Django accepted an offer to appear there with some misgiving, but found it to be exactly the right place for him. He was playing with musicians of a younger generation, such as the brothers Hubert and Raymond Fol on alto saxophone and piano respectively, trumpeter Bernard Hullin and bassist Pierre

Michelot. They had modern ideas and could fit in with his changing style without strain.

"They give me a hard time now and then," Django told his friend Pierre Fouad, "but I handed them a few new numbers, with difficult sequences, and they were all at sea. I got a bit of respect after that."

In fact, they had plenty of respect for him already. Raymond Fol noted the pleasure and relief that Django displayed as he settled in at the club, and contrasted these circumstances with the kind of surroundings in which he had been playing before. Fol laid the blame on "second-rate agents and managers", who had been concerned only with bookings and money. Now that he had found this new niche, Django went to extraordinary lengths to avoid falling by the wayside. He moved the family into the Hotel Montana, just across the street from the club, and scarcely stirred from Rue Benoît during the engagement. Coleridge Goode visited him at the hotel and discovered that he spent most of his time in bed.

"It was a sight to see," recalled Pierre Michelot, "when he came to the club in the evening. He was treated like a lord by his family, and a lord doesn't carry his own guitar. This was a job for his brother, or one of his cousins. Django would pick up his instrument, tune it in 30 seconds, since his ear was fantastic, and start to play – after turning his amplifier right up. He was so happy that everyone could hear him. It was a kind of revenge for years of frustration, for even with his powerful sound it was difficult to drown out the noise in a cabaret. Now all he had to do was turn a knob – and, early on, maybe he used it too much."

Recordings made with the Saint-Germain musicians are startlingly different from any of his previous work, but they throw a great deal of retrospective light on the last Grappelli sessions and the ones with the Quintette in its final form. We can now hear what Django had in mind. Both his themes and his solos are full of bebop phraseology, particularly in their use of the flattened fifth. Without going into theoretical explanations, suffice it to say that when a bebop line suddenly lands on a note that sounds as though it doesn't belong, it's probably a flattened fifth. (The last note of the eighth bar of 'Double Whisky', from the session of May 11th 1951, provides a vintage example.) This was the most noticeable element in the new harmonic thinking of Parker, Gillespie and co, in which the degree of dissonance was greatly increased and the choice of notes available to a soloist vastly expanded.

Time and familiarity have worn away its shock-value, but bebop derived much of its characteristic nervous edge from the use of 'screwy notes' like the flattened fifth. Django, of course, was purely an 'ear' player and unconcerned with the theoretical basis of the thing. He learned the bebop language as he had learned the language of swing, by listening and reproducing. As with his earlier style, the result was by no means an exact reproduction of the American original but something uniquely his own.

You have only to listen to the above-mentioned 'Double Whisky' to get a pretty good idea of how Django had arrived at this point. The three most obvious elements are: 'screwy notes'; passages played at double tempo; and quotation. His solo is packed with phrases that wander from the straight and narrow path of swing practice. Generally speaking, they are chromatic displacements, played a semitone above the expected pitch. Sometimes these are harmonically 'right' and sometimes they are not. The double tempo passages often sound spectacular from a technical point of view, although they have a tendency to tie themselves in knots. As for quotations, very popular in bebop circles, Django's solo begins with a long and obvious quote from 'Little White Lies', played in octaves. These three elements were all strongly represented in the playing of Dizzy Gillespie at the time, and Dizzy was the bebop master whom Django most admired.

> By late 1952 he had finally got a grip on the electric guitar

Hubert Fol, quoted by Charles Delaunay in his memoir of Django, summed it up very acutely: "Some evenings he was really fantastic, more perhaps because of the liberties he allowed himself to take – and only he could have got away with them – than because of the ideas he hit upon. Agreed, he was no bandleader, and his amplifier was always going wrong, but he was a personality. He had his own way of playing his own changes ... even for American tunes he didn't know and unconsciously fitted up with a harmonic sequence after his own lights."

There exists a somewhat scratchy live recording, made at the club, of 'Manoir de Mes Rêves', in which the new and old Django suddenly come together. The improvised line is as graceful as in the early days, but enriched with a touch of modern harmony, and the bebop influence does not sound stuck-on, as it often does in these later pieces. This suggests that Django might well have worked through the period of transition and digested the influence.

After the Saint-Germain residency, Django left to play the 1951 summer season at Knokke Casino, in Belgium. On his last night he had a phenomenal run of luck at the tables and left with his pockets stuffed full of money. Typically, he spent a large chunk of it on a taxi home to Paris. Having arrived back in style, he moved home yet again, to a little riverside house at Samois-sur-Seine, an idyllic spot on the edge of the Fôret de Fontainebleau. Here he spent his days fishing, painting and playing billiards in the local bar. Apart from an occasional week at the Club Saint-Germain or some other Paris club, and the odd guest spot, he gave every impression of having retired from the fray. But he could still be tempted by a big-band session for the radio. A few recordings from these have survived, notably two numbers with Aimé Barelli's orchestra – a version of Jerome Kern's 'Yesterdays', featuring some amazingly ornate guitar, and a ferociously fast and driving 'Lover'. These date from late 1952, by which time he really seems to have found his new direction, dropped the bebop clichés, and finally got a grip on the dynamics of the electric guitar.

At the beginning of 1953, Norman Granz, the American jazz impressario, arrived in Paris with his all-star travelling show, Jazz At The Philharmonic (JATP). Granz was in a completely different league from the managers and fixers Django had dealt with in the past. His tours were world-wide affairs, he paid better money than most jazz musicians had ever known, and all his artists travelled first-class. The two met backstage at a Paris concert and they discussed the possibility of Django joining JATP for a tour the following year. At Granz's suggestion, and possibly at his expense, Django recorded an album for the Blue Star label, to act as a 'calling card' for the projected tour. It turned out to be a revelation.

Although long-playing records (LPs) had been introduced in the late 1940s, and various compilations of Django's earlier work had come out in that format, this was the first (and, as it turned out, only) time he recorded a set of pieces specifically intended for LP release. The session took place on 10th March 1953, with Django as a featured soloist, accompanied by a young, modern rhythm section consisting of pianist Maurice Vander, bassist Pierre Michelot and drummer Jean-Louis Viale. With clean, bright mono recording, and plenty of studio time imparting a palpable sense of relaxation to the proceedings, this must at last be what Django had been aiming at over the past three or four years. The last vestiges of Hot Club style have gone, to be replaced with a clear, at times almost cool, improvised line over a lightly buoyant rhythm accompaniment.

The set of eight numbers includes a blues, two American classics, a French popular song, a Brazilian popular song, two Django favourites and Kurt Weill's 'September Song', which was written in the US but has a distinctly European, melancholy air about it. The first thing one notices is the comparative lack of ornate decoration in Django's playing. There is plenty of viruosity, but it stops short of that fill-every-corner hyperactivity to which he had been prone in earlier times. Almost certainly the reason is that he has finally got the measure of the electric guitar, in particular its capacity to sustain long notes. With the acoustic guitar, in average performing conditions, a guitar note decays quickly. The only way to deal with this, aside from cultivating the mandolin player's rapid tremolo, was to play a lot of notes. But now, in the benign acoustics of a recording studio, with a well-modulated rhythm section and a properly adjusted amplifier, he could let the notes ring, his theme statements in 'September Song' and 'Insensiblement' being perfect examples.

As we have seen, Django had made various attempts to get away from the rhythmic context established by the Quintette, but even doing away with the rhythm guitars did not achieve the change he was seeking. Only with the Club Saint-Germain band and, finally, the trio on the Blue Star album did he manage it, and then everything fell into place. His own improvised line became lighter, looser and less insistent. This, combined with the use of the electric guitar, had the effect of giving his style a slightly more 'American' feel, although no-one could be in any doubt that this was still Django Reinhardt.

There is a gentleness about his playing on the Blue Star session, especially in 'Nuages' and 'Manoir de mes Rêves', that some commentators, including musicians who knew him well, have interpreted as a presentiment of his approaching death. "As far as I am concerned," said Pierre Michelot, many years later, "this is the most beautiful version of 'Nuages' ever recorded. At one point he plays a phrase in such a way that it makes me shiver whenever I hear the record, and every time I hear it I'm touched. I couldn't say why. Did he have a premonition he was going to leave us? I don't know."

There was a further recording session in April, for Musidisc, with vibraphonist Fats Sadi. The results do not have quite the settled beauty of the Blue Star session, apart from a sweetly attractive version of the current French ballad 'Venez Donc Chez Moi'. After that, Django left for a short tour in Switzerland. While there, he complained of headaches and noticed that his fingers were swollen, but when Naguine urged him to see a doctor he dismissed the idea.

There are several differing versions of the circumstances surrounding Django's death. Some say he was fishing and collapsed on the riverbank. Others claim that he was at home, or taking a break in the local bar. The following is the version told by his son, Babik, aged nine at the time.

In the early hours of Saturday May 15th 1953, after playing at the Club Saint-Germain, Django walked to the Gare d'Austeritz. There he caught the early-morning train to Avon, the nearest station to Samois-sur-Seine, and walked back across the fields, a distance of about five kilometres. He stopped at the local café and was sitting on the terrace, sipping a cup of coffee, when he collapsed. It was a fine Saturday morning and it took longer than usual to locate a doctor. Django was rushed to hospital in Fontainebleau but died later that day without regaining consciousness.

Django Reinhardt lies buried in the grounds of the 11th century church at Samois-sur-Seine. His simple grave bears his name and the years of his birth and death: 1910-1953. His indifference to the written word followed him into eternity. On the grave his name was spelt 'Djengo'.

The legacy

THE 1950S WERE A GOLDEN AGE FOR JAZZ, in which its international audience grew to rival that for European classical music. Norman Granz both foresaw this and developed the means of exploiting it, through his Jazz At The Philharmonic tours and his record label, Clef. If Django had lived to take up Granz's offer he might have benefited enormously, both in financial terms (although that might have caused certain problems) and in the understanding of his music. As it was, he left behind a confused and incomplete picture which is only now becoming clear.

At the heart of the problem lay an apparent contradiction: Django was undoubtedly a jazz musician of near-genius, yet he was not an American. It just didn't add up, especially to Americans, who were rightly proud of jazz as an American art, the product of a unique and complex blend of musical cultures.

This bewilderment expressed itself in various ways. The trumpeter Doc Cheatham was quite candid about it: "Where did he learn to play like that? He wasn't playing American jazz, but he was swinging. It was upsetting to hear a man who was a foreigner swing like that!"

Others, during Django's lifetime, preferred to ignore that question altogether and go for what might be called the 'exotic outsider' angle. The most famous and oft-quoted of these is Gilbert McKean, who wrote a piece entitled 'The Fabulous Gipsy', which appeared in the June 1947 edition of *Esquire* magazine. It is instructive because the author seems blithely unaware of how insultingly racist his portrait of Django is: "Out of a welter of backward gipsy tribes with many almost medieval customs, the illiterate floating slum of the wagon train, has come this guitarist of gigantic creative stature." Which is roughly true, if disparaging to the Manouche people as a whole. It is the patronising tone that is really offensive:

"'*Attention*, my little cabbage,' he would exclaim to his wife. 'My sweet, it is time for me to go the job of music.'

"'*C'est bien*. I am ready, my love,' she would reply. Then she would bend forward, Django would mount her shoulders and off they would go through the mucky ways."

It is entirely possible that Naguine did carry Django, in his patent-leather dress shoes, over the occasional muddy patch – but 'my little cabbage'? If this was the view presented to American readers, it is hardly surprising that they were confused. But, whether it was the bemused admiration of Doc Cheatham, or McKean's condescension, the general view for many years was that Django Reinhardt was an isolated wonder, inexplicable, a curiosity. It was not until the 1960s that the perspective began to shift and, instead of listening to Django's music as a distorted reflection of American jazz, people started hearing it as a natural product of his own musical tradition, into which jazz had been incorporated.

The great American guitarist Barney Kessel was a first-generation disciple of Charlie Christian, the man who virtually invented the electric guitar as a jazz instrument and was its first and most influential exponent. Kessel admired Django greatly and struggled to find a formula to resolve the contradiction which his music posed. "To me, it's not really what I call jazz," he told the British writer Stan Britt in 1974. "It's improvised gipsy music. But definitely it has its place alongside jazz.

"The context in which he played was not straight-ahead jazz as I know it to be, but that does not prevent it from having great improvisational qualities. It's not his timing or the way he played. There were some things in his playing that, really, were not appropriate for jazz. The certain way he strummed, for instance. If he were playing with

The Gipsy genius in 1949, with a young admirer.

Count Basie or someone like that, it would not have grooved at all. He had enormous individuality but, to me, there were only tinges of jazz ... What I felt was a real Continental voice, a true European improviser. Actually, I think what he played is beyond jazz. It's in a separate category."

In the years since Kessel pondered this matter, his idea of jazz-beyond-jazz has turned out to be prophetic. Glancing quickly around the European jazz scene in the early 21st century, we come upon figures like Jan Garbarek, the Norwegian saxophonist and composer, with his combination of jazz, Nordic song and plainchant; the Dutchman Willem Breuker, who incorporates an element of hearty, village-square slapstick into his performances; and John Surman, a west-country Englishman with a choral background, whose jazz is filled with folksong, church music, brass bands, and so on. It was Surman himself who summed up the process in an interview in 2003: "Jazz started out as world music right back in New Orleans – it came in from all directions. It grew out of there because all the elements were there. It got distilled into a specific thing in the 1930s and 1940s, but now it's mushroomed out to be this huge thing."

> It was not long before other guitarists picked up Django's idiom

The phenomenon of jazz-beyond-jazz, of jazz merging with other musical idioms, is now widely recognised and accepted, but it had to start somewhere, and the most fertile ground for the first hybrid to take root was among the Gipsies of western Europe. In his delightful book, *Django's Gypsies*, Ian Cruickshank has this to say about the origins of their musical culture:

"Because of their ... exposure to the cultures of numerous countries encountered on their travels, the Gipsies have for centuries formed a gregarious musical subculture, which has encompassed many influences. The folk music of any area in which the Gipsies lived would be immediately improvised upon, and then assimilated, in a most exciting and original way, into their own music. As a result, the Gipsies were usually the most sought-after musicians in many parts of Europe by the ruling classes."

When Django Reinhardt first encountered jazz, he instinctively followed this traditional practice. He absorbed the idiom of Armstrong and Ellington and worked it into a fabric of his own design. The difference was that, instead of being a local folk music, jazz was a popular idiom disseminated around the world by mass media, a kind of global folk music. The industrialisation of entertainment was ensuring that it was no longer the exclusive property of one culture or one race or one nation. Similarly, when Django began making records his music could be heard anywhere, and it was not long before other guitarists were picking up the idiom he had evolved.

The process began with his immediate circle. Read the personnel on any CD compilation of music by the classic Quintette du Hot Club de France and you will find at least one of the surnames Reinhardt, Ferret (or Ferré) and Vées. The families were related and full of musicians, and they were attached by ties of kinship and culture to other families of musicians. Django's notorious practice of sending along one of his cousins to take his place, and the ease with which any one of them could step into the rhythm guitar role with the Quintette, shows how quickly and efficiently they had cottoned on to his music. Before long, Gipsy musicians all over Europe were playing Django-style and passing it down through the generations. The names Escoudé, Lagrene, Winterstein, Lafertin, Rosenberg and others recur regularly in the lists of Gipsy players. Almost always, they start at a very young age. Birelli Lagrene, from Alsace, began playing professionally at eleven and released his first album at 14. Stochelo Rosenberg, from the Netherlands, began at around the same age, and his brother, Jimmy, even younger.

Gipsy musicians continue to play homage to Django. Every year since 1981, and irregularly before that, a jazz festival has been held over several days in June at Samois-sur-Seine. Although other types of jazz are to be heard, it is still essentially a Gipsy gathering. The music played is by no means a strict reproduction of Django's style. Indeed, strict adherence to any orthodoxy would be against the whole nature of Gipsy music, but the sheer diversity of styles epitomises the culture from which his music sprang.

The Quintette du Hot Club de France existed, in its classic form, only for about five years, and even then it was a somewhat on-and-off affair. Yet its distinctive sound has become a kind of aural shorthand for France in the 1930s and the war years. Snatches are forever being played behind television commercials and travelogues, radio programmes and the occasional feature film. A particularly effective example of the latter is Louis Malle's *Lacombe Lucien* (1974), set

during the occupation. The evocative quality of the Quintette's sound is as powerful as that of Glenn Miller's music, and for similar reasons: it is instantly recognisable, unambiguously attached to a time and place, and vastly nostalgic – even to people too young to remember the period.

The Quintette shares something else with Glenn Miller, too, namely a posthumous career that seems set to last indefinitely. Not only do its records, endlessly repackaged, continue to sell in healthy quantities, but the world is full of latter-day Quintettes, playing the music – or an approximation to it – live. It is hard to say when this began, but one of the earliest and most authentic recreations must have been Diz Disley's Soho String Quintet of the late 1950s. Disley, a British guitarist of great charm and determination, as well as talent, eventually came closest of all to reviving the Quintette, by reintroducing Stéphane Grappelli to the format he had helped to create, and successfully touring the world with him in the 1970s and 1980s.

Nowadays, the style of the Quintette is so popular, with so many bands striving to emulate the sound of the original, that it has become a recognised subdivision of jazz, known as 'Hot Club'. There is swing and hard bop and Latin-jazz and Dixieland – and Hot Club. Bands consisting of violin, two or three guitars and bass are to be found everywhere. They are especially popular in France, of course, where the style is still called 'swing', but also in Scandinavia (Svenska Hotkvintett, Hot Club de Norvège), Australia (Monsieur Camembert), the USA (Billets Doux, Hotclub Sandwich), and even Japan (Swing Nights). Very occasionally someone attempts to build something new on the old foundations. The most successful so far has been Martin Taylor's Spirit Of Django, which flourished briefly in the mid-1990s and created a genuinely original and Django-esque patchwork of styles and textures.

What Django himself would have made of all this is hard to imagine. He would probably have been baffled to find so many people emulating the "little orchestra, without drums or trumpets" that he had created with Grappelli in the 1930s. At the time of his death he had already liberated himself from what he found to be the constrictions of the Hot Club style and was heading in a quite different direction. We know he longed to compose orchestral music, and even started work on a Mass. If he had lived to be as old as Grappelli he might have created symphonies through the medium of Gérard Lévêque and his long-suffering successors. Or he might have spent the time in fishing and playing billiards. One thing is certain – he would have done exactly as he liked.

Following Django's death, the press was filled with the kind of high-flown eulogies with which the French honour their dead artists. The writer Jean Cocteau, for instance, compared him to "one of those gentle fauns, who die in captivity", a "sacred and wandering soul", and so on.

But it was Django's son, Babik (an accomplished guitarist himself, who died in 2001), who would later express it most simply and movingly: "My father was certainly a giant in the world of jazz and all his admirers know that he was a Gipsy ... His behaviour sometimes appeared strange to people who were not Gipsies. Of course, true geniuses behave differently from the rest of us. But, above all, my father was a Gipsy."

ABOVE LEFT Django's last home, at Samois-sur-Seine, on the edge of the Fôret de Fontainebleau. BELOW LEFT A memorial plaque on the house. It reads, "Here lived and died the guitarist and composer Django Reinhardt 1910-1953." RIGHT Since Django's death, Samois-sur-Seine has become a place of annual pilgrimage for admirers and players of Gipsy jazz .

Django Reinhardt
THE MUSIC

Django's guitar

It is rare in the guitar world for a player to be linked throughout his career with just one company, let alone just one type of guitar. Yet, by a series of coincidences, a classical guitarist and luthier with little knowledge of the jazz world was to design a guitar that gradually evolved to become the only guitar Django Reinhardt was ever to endorse. The vast majority of his recordings and concerts were performed on this one model, and by association it has become the first choice for guitarists around the world seeking that elusive Gipsy-jazz authenticity.

MARIO MACCAFERRI

In 1930 Mario Maccaferri was well known across Europe as a classical guitarist, having given recitals in his native Italy and in France, Switzerland and Germany. As a young man he had been apprenticed to the instrument maker Luigi Mozzani in his hometown of Cento. He had learned to make guitars, harp-guitars, mandolins, violins and other stringed instruments, while simultaneously studying the guitar. He had been living in London for two years, teaching and giving the occasional concert or touring. In his spare time he had built a few prototypes of experimental guitars, intended to improve the range and projection of the instrument, no doubt spurred on by the need to be heard at the back of the larger concert halls.

He believed that contact between the player's body and the back of the guitar robbed the guitar of its tone, and devised a two part structure to fit inside the guitar and resonate unhindered by contact with the player. Firstly there was an inner box that fitted closely inside the back and sides of the lower bout of the guitar, with an opening where it faced the soundhole. There was then added a 'reflector' that curved from the back of the guitar towards the opposite side of the soundhole, so that sound emerging through the box opening would be reflected out through the soundhole. This internal soundbox and reflector are the reason for the characteristic large D-shaped soundhole on the original Maccaferri design.

THE SELMER MACCAFERRI

In 1931, Maccaferri, an astute businessman as well as a musician and inventor, showed his plans to Ben Davis, the manager of the Selmer shop in London. He in turn suggested a meeting with Henri Selmer in Paris to discuss setting up a workshop at the Selmer factory to manufacture guitars under Maccaferri's direction. As a classical player, the designer's main interest was in gut-stringed guitars, but Davis was keen to compete with his business rivals who were importing steel-stringed Epiphones, Gibsons and Martins from the USA. As he ran a shop frequented

The Maccaferri-designed Selmer Orchestre guitar of 1932, also known as the Jazz.

by all the best jazz players in England he was also aware of the shift away from banjo towards guitar in jazz groups. Seeing a business opportunity, he requested that the product line be expanded to include steel-stringed instruments.

In seeking inspiration for this additional guitar, Mario turned to the mandolin, an instrument he knew to be loud relative to its size and capable of good articulation and response. He took some elements of guitar design – eg, an arched top – and combined them with the bent down shape that was traditional in mandolin design, where the top angles toward the back of the instrument behind the bridge, which is held in place by the downward pressure of the strings, rather than glued. The soundbox and reflector were part of this guitar design too, which meant it also had the D-shaped soundhole.

Manufacturing guitars in the 1930s was a semi-industrial process. Lathes and cutting machines were used to prepare wood and metal parts, and dies needed to be made for stamping out parts such as the bent metal tailpiece and tuner covers.

Workers at Selmer, world leaders in brass and woodwind instruments, were experienced in both metalwork and woodwork and Maccaferri had supervised production in Mozzani's workshop as a young man. Production quickly gathered pace during 1931 and the first guitars were shipped in 1932, almost all going to London.

The level of commitment from the Selmer Company to its new role of guitar maker is shown by the inclusion of no fewer than five models in the catalogue in that first year.

THE GUITARS

The guitars fall neatly into two types. There were the classical models, intended for gut strings, which were called Concert, Espagnol and Classique. Then there were two steel string models: the Orchestre (later known as the Jazz) and the Hawaiian. All were marked inside 'Henri Selmer, Paris', initially by means of a bakelite plate; later a label was glued to the inside of the guitar showing the model name and serial number. The Selmer logo was also engraved on the face of the headstock along with one of Maccaferri's various patent numbers.

Selmer's Modèle Jazz of 1936, created after the departure of Maccaferri

The Concert

The Concert model closely resembled the more famous Orchestre or Jazz model, and was probably the design closest to Maccaferri's personal idea of guitar heaven. The body was larger than usual for a classical guitar and of a shape entirely the designer's own, partly to give a greater volume but also to make room for the inner soundbox. It had a deep cutaway to the 15th fret, a feature that is not universally accepted on classical guitars even today. The heel was flat where the neck joins the body, rather than pointed as normal. There were 12 frets to the body on the wide flat ebony fingerboard, with 24 frets under the high E string accommodated by an extension over the large D soundhole.

The head, neck and heel were made from three pieces of walnut and glued together with the head and neck strengthened by a curved tongue-like tenon joint under the fingerboard. The wider than usual glued-down classical style bridge was made of ebony and had a two-part saddle to improve intonation. The internal 'fan' strutting of this guitar was similar to the normal practice for classical guitars, and the European spruce top was flat, without the arch of the jazz model. There was a distinctive trapezoid headstock with an ebony veneer and a zero fret, the latter being common to all the guitars in the range.

The Espagnol

This guitar had a more conventional appearance, without the large D soundhole or cutaway, and had a conventional classical headstock. In other respects it retained the other essential features of the Concert. The soundbox was modified to allow for the smaller round soundhole.

The Classique

Maccaferri or Selmer seems to have decided that a conventional guitar was essential to complete the range, and this guitar had none of the innovation of the others. It was a standard classical instrument in every respect.

The Orchestre

This was the instrument that came to be known as the Jazz model. It was the same shape and size as the Concert though it could be ordered without a cutaway. There were 24 frets on the same fingerboard extension and the same flat heel. It also had the internal soundbox, D soundhole and three-piece neck. Four lateral struts replaced the fan bracing of the 'classical' Concert model and a central strut was added to strengthen the glue joint where the two halves of the top met.

The arch in the spruce top was obtained by curving the struts and then gluing the top to fit; the guitar was not an 'arch-top' in the sense of being carved like a typical 1930s arch-top guitar. The top was bent down behind the bridge, mandolin style, and the back and sides were usually made from a three-ply combination of mahogany on the inside and rosewood on the outside. The centre laminate was usually poplar, laid with its grain at a right angle to the outer woods. Maccaferri had discovered that correctly made plywood can be both strong and light, although today it is often wrongly associated only with cheap guitars.

The strings were attached to the mandolin-style tailpiece screwed to the bottom of the guitar, which could take either loop or ball end strings. The bridge was not glued but held in place by the downward pressure of the strings and had wooden extensions either side, which were glued in place and helped with location as well as being decorative. The slotted headstock of the Concert model, with its trapezoid shape, was still present but the tuner spindles were made of steel to take the steel strings. Maccaferri's innovative tuners were encased in a screwed down box, protecting them and ensuring a tight fit, and the teeth of the cogs were cut at an angle so that more were in contact with the gear. The mechanism was lubricated permanently at the point of manufacture; these features have since become standard on modern manufacturers' tuners.

The Hawaiian

A modified version of the Orchestre model was made to satisfy the demand for guitars that could be played flat on the lap with a steel bar. Hawaiian music was very popular in the USA, and had also caught on in France and Britain. The soundbox was retained, but the cutaway was removed as unnecessary. The strings are held off the fingerboard by a high nut, the frets serving only as markers. A seven-string version was offered, but it is essentially the same as the six-string with a larger nut to take the extra string and four tuners on the top side of the headstock.

New Models

In the following year some new models were added to the range, including a harp guitar with three extra strings (Maccaferri was a devotee), a four-string tenor guitar, the four-string tenor 'Grand-Modèle' and the Eddie Freeman guitar, which attempted to modify the tuning of a tenor banjo to obtain the sonority of a guitar. The latter guitar is noteworthy only in that it specifically excluded the soundbox as inefficient.

SUCCESS AND FAILURE

It is fair to say that the range as a whole was not a success. Players did not take to the inner soundbox, which seemed to choke the dynamics of the classical models and contributed little to the steel string models. It did give the classical guitars a very even response throughout their range, but considering the additional time and expense it caused during manufacture its inclusion in the design could hardly be justified. No more than a few dozen of most of the models were made, the exception being the Orchestre model, with up to 200 being shipped to England in the first years, where they were cautiously adopted by some prominent players. The Eddie Freeman was made in some numbers, though any surviving examples tend to have been converted to 6-string use.

If sales were slow in England, however, they began to pick up in France, not least because a certain guitar playing sensation, Django Reinhardt, had discovered the guitar and been widely photographed playing it. As the Quintette du Hot Club de France became more and more famous, so did the Selmer guitars with which it was associated. 1934 was the year the Quintette made its recording breakthrough, but by then Maccaferri had severed all connection with the Selmer Company and with the guitar that he had designed.

SELMER WITHOUT MACCAFERRI

During the course of 1933, a dispute developed between Maccaferri and Henri Selmer. Its full details can only be guessed at, but the designer was unhappy with certain clauses in his contract, and Selmer may have been unhappy with the guitarist's interest in other aspects of his business. (Maccaferri later founded a highly successful woodwind reed-making business in America, competing directly with Selmer.) Production was well established in the guitar workshop and could continue without the designer's presence, but there were some immediate problems, not least that Maccaferri had taken out patents on his soundbox design and it could no longer be used without his permission. The result was that during the years 1934 to 1936 the exact appearance of the Selmer guitar varied widely. D-holes, round holes and small oval holes, classical and trapezoid headstocks, cutaway and non-cutaway bodies, and 12- and 14-fret necks all appeared on these guitars in random order. Output fell steeply and gut-stringed models were discontinued.

The new Modèle Jazz

During the course of 1936 a standard guitar was gradually developed which was to remain in production, apart from a few years during the war, until 1952. The D-hole was gone for good, as was the soundbox and the 12-fret neck join. Players had come to expect a 14-fret neck, which together with the cutaway gave excellent high fret access. The original shape tailpiece, bridge and headstock were kept, but a small oval soundhole replaced the now unnecessary D-hole. The fingerboard extension was discontinued and 21 frets were fixed to the board, which ended curved round the oval soundhole. The same woods were used as before, although there are occasional minor variations particularly during wartime.

Django had publicised the Orchestre model and continued to be photographed with the new Jazz model. Over the years he was to own and play many Selmers, as in exchange for his support he was encouraged to visit the Selmer shop and equip himself and his musicians as he wished. Guitars were often subsequently given away to friends, family and colleagues. However he eventually settled on one particular instrument, number 503, made in 1940, and kept it until his death in 1953. In 1964 Django's wife Naguine donated this guitar to the Cité de la Musique, Paris, where it can still be seen.

In 1939, hoping to exploit Django's growing success and association with the Jazz model, Selmer began to inscribe 'Modèle Django Reinhardt' on the face of the headstock between the string slots. This was mostly in flowing script, but some, including Django's own No 503, just have 'Django Reinhardt' in capitals. These guitars are in every other respect standard Jazz models, however, and the practice was discontinued within a year. The only other variation on the now established Jazz model was when a maple neck with a flat, rather than slotted, headstock was fitted to a run of about 20 guitars during the years 1941 to 1942. These guitars also had maple bodies and may well be the result of shortages of the usual materials due to the war. Some guitars made near to the end of production can be found with rosewood necks.

THE DEMAND FOR COPIES

By 1952, guitar production was a minute and irrelevant part of the activity of the Selmer company and the decision was taken to shut down production. The entire contents of the guitar workshop were sold to the Paris-based luthier Jean Beuscher. Many unfinished or damaged guitars were completed or repaired in his workshop, and many parts were sold to other makers to be used on copies. In fact, the Selmer copy industry was already well under way in France, with many independent builders, often of Italian extraction, offering Selmer-inspired instruments often at more affordable prices. Busato and Di Mauro were among the most prolific imitators, though their instruments are rarely exact copies and tend instead to have Selmer-like features such as the abrupt cutaway and the oval soundhole.

In the early 1970s, the English publisher and instrument importer Maurice Summerfield arranged for around 1,300 Selmer copies to be made in Japan for the UK market and sold under the CSL brand. These were good quality instruments and have since become valued by guitarists. All had 12-fret necks but both D and oval soundholes were featured. In 1979 he instigated a further run of about 400 D-hole guitars under the Ibanez brand, this time with Maccaferri's approval and signature on each one, until Maccaferri became unhappy with the quality of the product and refused to sign any more labels. Japan's Saga company was next in line, with a series more closely based on the Selmer tradition, including both 12-fret D-hole and 14-fret oval hole guitars. Thanks to the spread of Django's music around the world and to his many followers there are now countless makers producing copies of varying levels of accuracy.

THE SELMER LEGACY

The Selmer company made guitars for just 20 years and probably produced fewer than 1000 instruments in that time, mostly steel-string guitars of a type not really intended by the original designer. That they were innovative is beyond dispute, and though many of the features that go together to make a Selmer can be found individually on other guitars it is the combination of headstock, tuners, body shape, woods and construction methods that makes them unique both in appearance and sound quality.

Most guitar builders would not set out to create an instrument with the qualities of the Selmer Maccaferri. The bass is powerful without being boomy, the treble can be incisive or sweet, depending how the guitar is played. The deep cutaway and fast shallow neck cry out for a virtuoso to exploit the entire fingerboard, but in the wrong hands its immediacy of attack and responsiveness can sound dry and brittle. A strong vibrato is required to preserve its sustain, though its saving grace is its ability to project; since the only way for Django to amplify his guitar in the early 1930s was to play into a microphone he seems to have appreciated this quality more than any other.

The Selmer captures the spirit of the age in which it was invented, and has become a design icon in much the same way as the Fender Stratocaster or Gibson Les Paul. One photo on a CD cover conjures up the era of swing, of Gipsy jazz, of 1930s Paris and London, when guitarists were emerging from the rhythm section to play single note and chord solos at the front of the band. The Selmer Maccaferri grew out of the same need for loudness that, across the Atlantic, had created the Martin Dreadnought and the Dobro Resonator; guitars which have also found their 'niche' (in bluegrass and blues) because of qualities that in other fields would be viewed as faults. Mario Maccaferri never met Django, and Django was a phenomenon on any guitar, but it is fortunate for us all that the Selmer came along at exactly the right time for Django to explore his creativity to its limits, and in doing so to create and popularise an entire genre of music.

Play like Django

ANYONE LISTENING TO DJANGO REINHARDT play on the classic Hot Club recordings can probably tell he was one of the most remarkable guitarists there has ever been. Even a casual look through the transcriptions in this book will confirm the extent of his mastery of both the guitar and the improvisation that is essential to the Gypsy jazz style. Is it possible to play like him? The fact that it is not going to be easy does not discourage thousands of people around the world from enjoying the attempt. With some guidance, based on careful analysis of what Django actually does, it is possible to play some great, and stylistically appropriate music.

THE SOUND

A steel stringed acoustic guitar is ideal, and though it does not have to be a Selmer-style guitar it does need to be suitable for plectrum playing. A fairly high action is preferable, for a clean buzz-free sound and lots of dynamic range, though the strings don't need to be particularly heavy. Django used 'Argentines' which are relatively light and have a soft silver-plated copper wrap on a steel core, lending them a responsive but mellow quality. Use a stiff pick and get used to playing nearer the bridge than normal for an incisive tone, moving nearer the neck for the warmer tones needed for ballads and those expressive moments. Ideally you should keep your whole picking hand off the guitar, moving freely from the whole wrist and arm rather than resting the fingers on the guitar top. You should also aim to pick virtually every note, as Django uses relatively few hammer-ons and pull-offs (or slurs, as they will be called from now on). For the left hand, apart from strength, speed, agility and co-ordination, an intense vibrato would be useful. Concentrate on 'wiggling' the string from side to side very rhythmically to develop this.

DJANGO'S TRICKS

Mastering a few of the following will make your playing more authentic; they also come in handy if you run out of melodic inspiration.

Rakes and sweeps

Here's a simple sweep from 'Minor Swing', bar 36:

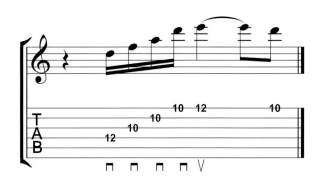

Hold the first 4 notes down and play them with one downstroke across four strings, then add the last note with an upstroke.

This one from 'Bouncin' Around' is less easy, though again you need to start with the fingers down on the E and A strings before making a quick jump to the D, G, and B strings and sliding down one fret to arrive on E. Use one downstroke across all five strings. Good luck!

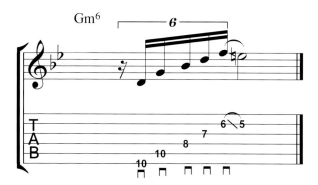

Bends

Most of Django's bends are of one semitone. In 'Minor Swing' (bar 73) the 5th of A minor is bent up to the flattened 6th and released:

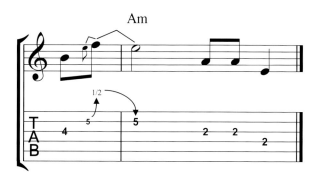

The sharp 4th is often bent up to the 5th, as in 'Sweet Chorus', bar 12:

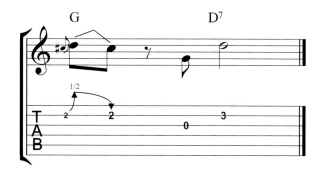

In 'Minor Swing', bar 59, the minor 3rd of D minor is bent up to the major 3rd, F#:

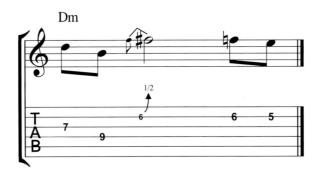

You will find many other examples in the following pages.

Octaves

Django plays octaves in two ways, with either a one-string gap or a two-string gap, with the middle strings muted with the left hand. Both are illustrated here:

'Djangology' bars 53-57

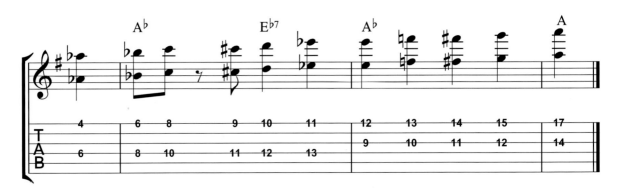

'Minor Swing' bars 77-78

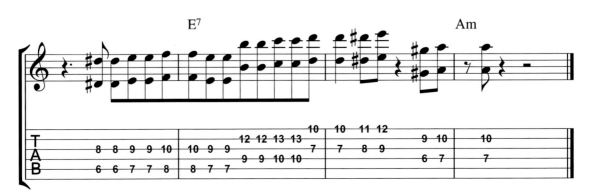

Octaves are a powerful sound; use downstrokes for the downbeats in the first version, and alternate down and up strokes in the second.

Glissandi

You can slide along the frets to a new note in either upward or downward directions, and you can pick the note again when you arrive or not. Django's playing is full of subtle and expressive glissandi of all types; here is an excerpt from 'Djangology' (bars 42-44) that demonstrates just a few.

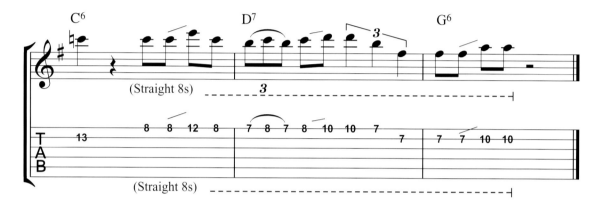

Tremolando or tremolo picking

Essentially this technique is the creation of a sustained sound by means of very fast alternate picking. Django uses this on chords, particularly when accompanying Grappelli's solos, such as in 'Sweet Chorus', bars 48-49:

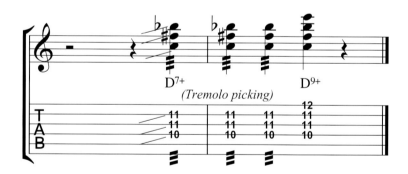

Tremolo glissando

As well as the regular glissandi mentioned above, Django sometimes applies tremolando picking as he slides, creating a romantic mandolin-like 'sostenuto'. This can be heard in this example also taken from 'Sweet Chorus', bars 16-18:

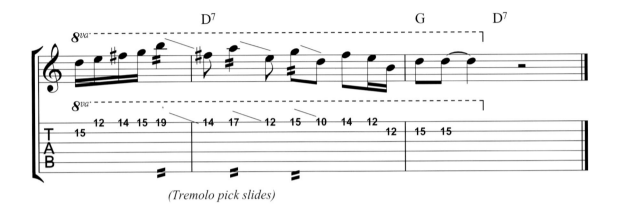

(Tremolo pick slides)

Fast chromatics

Django uses just one finger when playing fast chromatic scales, co-ordinating tremolo picking (as above) with the glissando-like movement over the frets. Here's a particularly impressive example from 'Bouncin' Around':

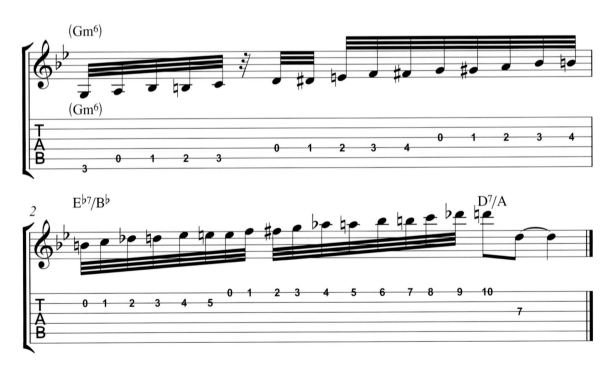

HARMONY/MELODY

All the above are in the end just tricks, however, and without a good understanding of the melodic possibilities of the chords of a song you're going to be left without any true substance to your improvisation. Here's an analysis of Django's playing from a harmony viewpoint.

Arpeggios

Generally speaking Django does not use scales at all. The odd melodic passage may refer to a scale but his runs are based on arpeggios. (An arpeggio is a chord played one note at a time.) If the chord is minor, use the minor 6th arpeggio and emphasise the 6th. This example is from 'Djangology', bar19:

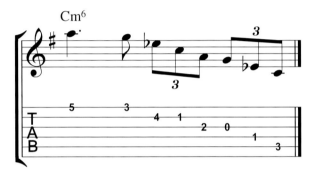

If the chord is major, use the major 6th arpeggio, emphasise the 6th and add the 9th occasionally too ('Djangology', bar 111):

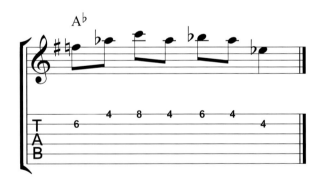

If the chord is a 7th, Django sometimes uses a 9th chord arpeggio as in this example, also from 'Djangology', bar 30:

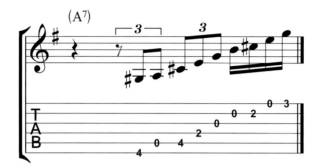

Frequently on a 7th chord Django builds a diminished 7th arpeggio on the 3rd, 5th, or 7th of the chord and uses that, as in this extract from 'Djangology', bar 18:

Note that Django often plays arpeggios with some open strings.

In a minor key, with songs such as 'Minor Swing' and 'Bouncin' Around', the above substitution will give you notes from the harmonic minor scale, for that authentic Gypsy flavour.

It is important to remember to play melodically and not slavishly follow the chords with one arpeggio after another. One way of making arpeggios sound more melodically interesting is the 'decorated arpeggio'. Here you play a note above or below, or both, before or after playing the chord tone, as in these examples from 'Minor Swing':

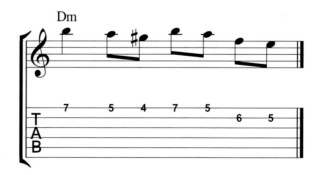

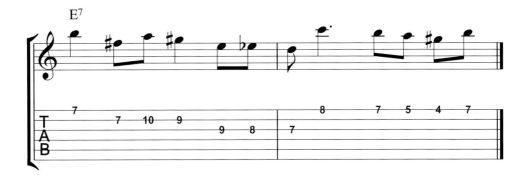

Django does not use 'box' shapes like blues scales, though he does like the sound of the flattened third as in 'Djangology', bar 16:

Finally, make a conscious effort to use the whole guitar, for example by playing 'call and response' phrases in alternately high and low registers, as in several places in 'Bouncin' Around'.

RHYTHM GUITAR

If all this is too much for you, stick with the hard plectrum and the high action and play rhythm. At its most fundamental, Hot Club rhythm guitar is like a pile driver hitting all four beats in a bar, each slightly staccato and with a slight accent on the second and fourth beats. Make no attempt to play any eighth-notes at all. Variations on this can be heard in 'Minor Swing' and the much more expansive and 'filled in' 'Bouncin' Around'. Use the kinds of chord shape found in the following pages, avoiding the bland bar-chords that guitarists so often fall into using. With careful listening, the rhythm parts can be heard quite clearly on the CD, so just play along and imitate.

Which brings us to the most important piece of advice of all: to listen. Keep going back to the CD and listen to the tone, the phrasing, the notes, the accompaniment and anything else you can think of. Learning to listen makes us all better musicians. Play along with the solos and then try making up your own in the spaces left for the violin solos. If you like what you hear, do it some more; if you don't, experiment until you find something you do like. There are no rules, so just be guided by your own taste and experience. That, after all, is how Django learned.

The Transcriptions

In this section of the book you will find complete song transcriptions of six important Django Reinhardt recordings. There are two medium tempo tunes, one in a major key and one minor, and two slower tunes, again one major and one minor. The fifth tune is 'Honeysuckle Rose', a fast tempo example of the Quintette's ability at interpreting the work of other composers, and the sixth is the classic 'Nuages', representing the later wartime period of recordings without Stéphane Grappelli.

NOTATION

All of these tunes feature sections in 'swing' time, and some have sections in 'straight' time too. Both 'feels' are notated the same, but in 'swing' the quavers are played as the outer two of a triplet (below). If you find this confusing just listen to the enclosed CD and copy what you hear.

TABLATURE

The usual 'tab' conventions are followed, rhythms being found only on the notation stave. Fingerings have not been included, as Django's own fingerings are rarely appropriate for the four-fingered guitarist. It is possible, however, to play all of Django's single-note guitar parts as found in the tab with just fingers one and two, and trying this can reveal a deeper understanding of his style. For example, using only the strongest two fingers of the fretting hand can produce a more powerful tone than that produced with fingers three and four by the normal player. Also certain arpeggio shapes become more logical when this fingering limitation is applied. Try it: you may wish to alter the tab to suit in some places. Remember that a note can be found one string lower by moving five frets higher, except between the G and B strings, where the interval is four frets.

Slurs

Play the first note with the pick and sound the others with the left hand by pulling-off or hammering-on as appropriate.

Slides or glissandi

These are notated using a straight line (below). Play the first note and slide along the string holding it down against the frets.

Tremolando

This is rapid alternate picking, either on single notes or on chords (above right).

Double bars mark the ends of sections. These are usually, but not always, eight bars in length. The tab for each song is followed by a chord chart showing the basic structure, with diagrams showing the chord shapes as played by the rhythm guitarists. The chord name above the staves refer to this underlying harmony, rather than to the passing harmony generated by the soloist. Where Django plays chords as part of his solo their names are shown between the guitar staves to avoid confusion. All rhythm chords are assumed to be in root position. 'Slash' chords are used where this is not the case. For example, D7/A means a D7 chord with A in the bass.

Djangology

In this tune, fittingly named for the study of all things Django, the guitarist takes us on a romp through a selection from his endless repertoire of guitar effects and tricks. The whole piece is characterised by fast arpeggios and the free use of the entire fingerboard. We also find rapid alternate picking (bars 28/29 and 36/37), the occasional 'rake' or sweep (bars 30 and 59), 'tremolo picking' slides (bar 114) and regular slides or 'glisses' both up and down. Django also throws in some chord fills (bars 56 and 62) and a passage in octaves.

INTRODUCTION

First, however we are treated to a virtuoso display of parallel arpeggios on guitar and violin, based only loosely on the chords of the theme. The first two bars are based on A9, followed by Cmaj13 with an F#, (suggesting the Lydian #11) provided by the violin. For jazz in 1935, this is impressively modern. Bbdim7 then leads to an F#7 chord in bar 6, which is the start of a chromatic descent passing through a held F7, to arrive on E major in bar 9. We have come a long way from the opening chord of A7 and the home key of G major is still nowhere in sight. The solo guitar then brings us first to B7, then chromatically again to Bb7 and finally back to A7, and the start of the theme, though the melody is only hinted at in the first eight bars as Django improvises freely throughout his choruses.

STRUCTURE

There is an eight bar 'A' section, which is repeated, with a 'B' section followed by once more through the 'A'. This is a common form for jazz and popular songs of the time and is often referred to as 'AABA'. Each time through the form is called a 'chorus'. Normally the B section would be the same length as the A, but here it is only four bars, giving a length of 28 bars for the whole chorus. Django and Stéphane take two choruses each, but in the final chorus Django takes the 'B' section, leaving Steph to finish the last eight bars. The opening arpeggios then come back, modified to end on a held F#dim7 in bar 128 before the arrival back on G and the conclusion with Django's guitar harmonics. It's worth noting that the violin notes at the end can only be played on a guitar with at least 23 frets. (An early D-hole Maccaferri, with 24, would do nicely.) The best alternative is to take the last four notes down an octave.

RHYTHM GUITAR

Django was capable of coming up with strange and quirky chord sequences; 'Rhythm Futur' or 'Black and White' spring to mind but there are many examples to choose from. There is something so right and logical about this one, however, that it is easy to ignore its originality. Note how the shapes flow from one to the next on the fingerboard; there is deep guitar logic in this unusual progression. It also reveals how Django was able to play fully fleshed out rhythm parts despite the injury to his left hand. The notes on the sixth and fourth strings are played with fingers one or two, whilst the injured fingers three or four are wedged in to play the G string. The Ab and A major chords in the B section would be played 'thumb over', ie, with the left hand thumb holding down the low E string, a technique which Django used a great deal to compensate for the lack of flexibility in his third and fourth fingers.

HARMONY AND ANALYSIS

In soloing on this tune Django begins with a melodic idea based on the arpeggio of the A7 chord in the accompaniment, rising to the 9th, B natural. He repeats the B over the Cm6 chord too; the strength of the melodic invention makes light of such dissonances. As usual arpeggios tend to be favoured over scales; C#dim7 is regularly used over the A7 chords (resulting in an A7b9 harmony) and Cm6 arpeggios occur in bars 11, 19, 47 but other devices include chromatic fragments (bars 15 and 22) and the use of the 'blues' minor 3rd, Bb, over the G major chord in bars 16 and 24. Django also puts in some of his trademark decorative turns, based on notes above and below a chord tone, such as those in bars 33, 41, 48, etc. Notice also how in bars 16/17, and more obviously in bars 33/35, he creates tension by repeating the same short phrase again and again over the descending chord sequence. Django imitators hoping to develop their 'two-finger' ability should look closely at bars 28-29, a classic Django lick played with rapid alternate pick strokes and just fingers one and two.

For its variety, breadth of expression and sheer effortless mastery, Djangology is a very worthwhile subject for study.

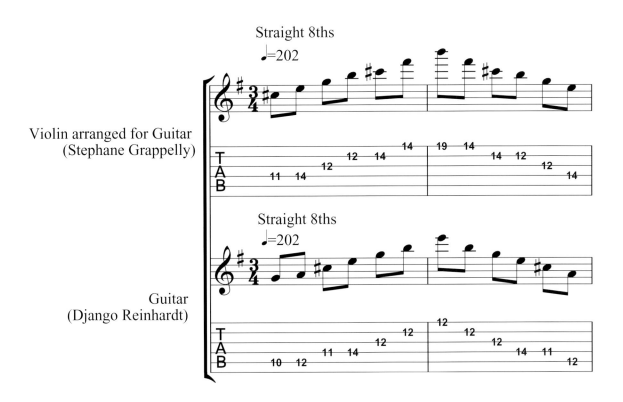

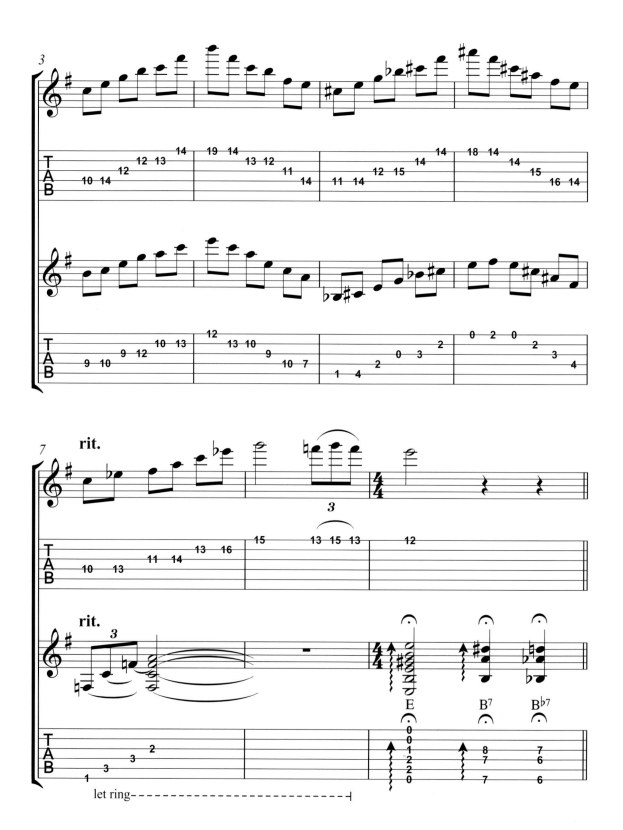

Guitar Solo:
Swing 8ths

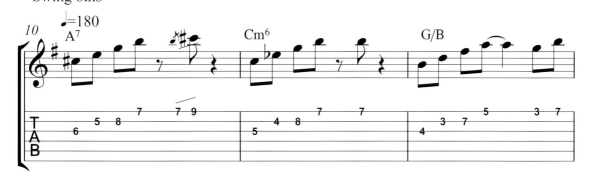

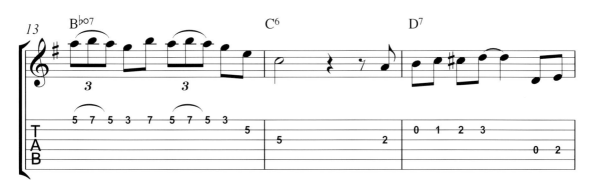

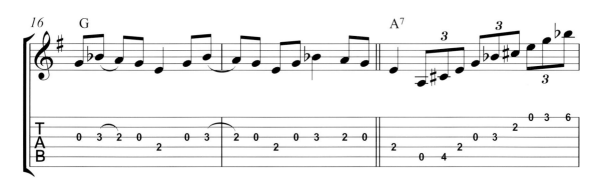

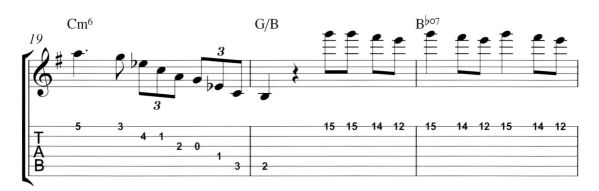

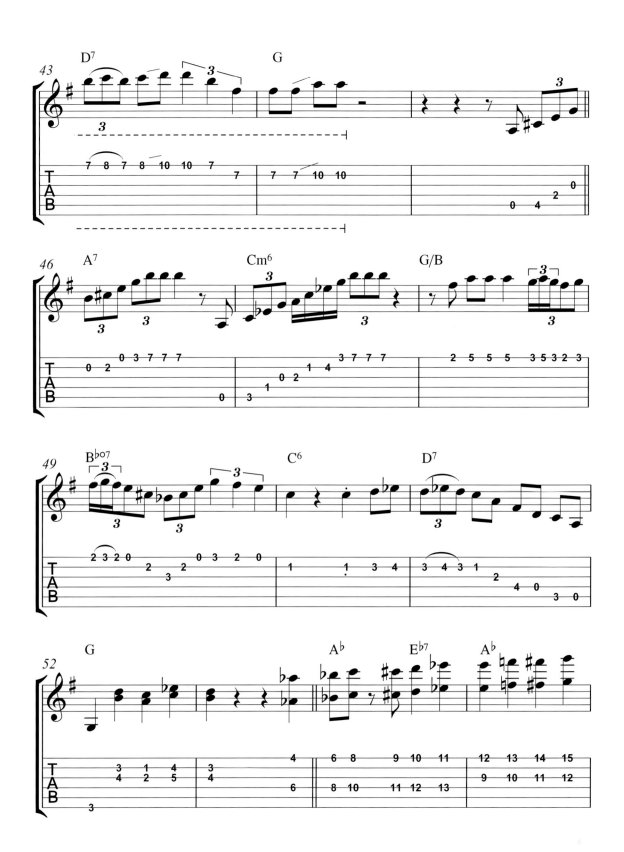

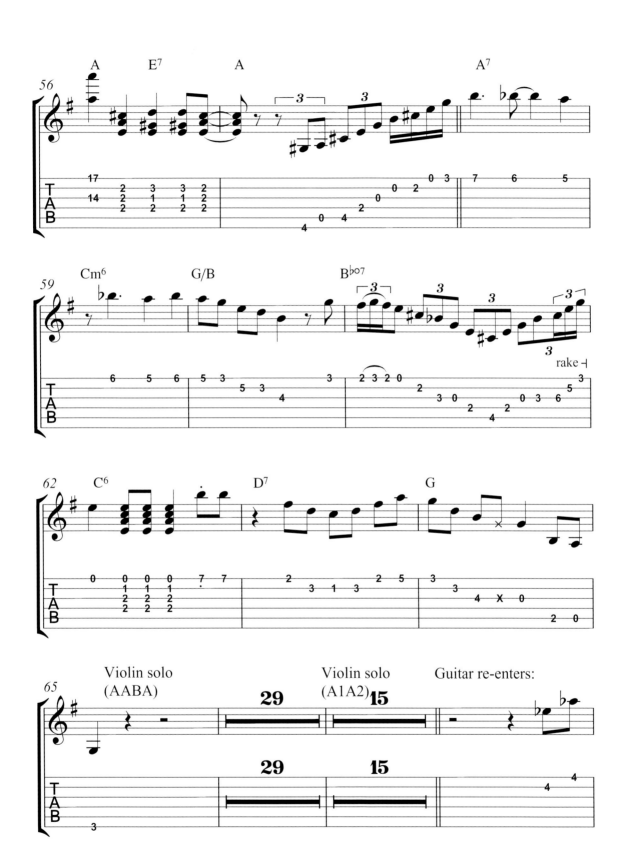

DJANGOLOGY CHORDS

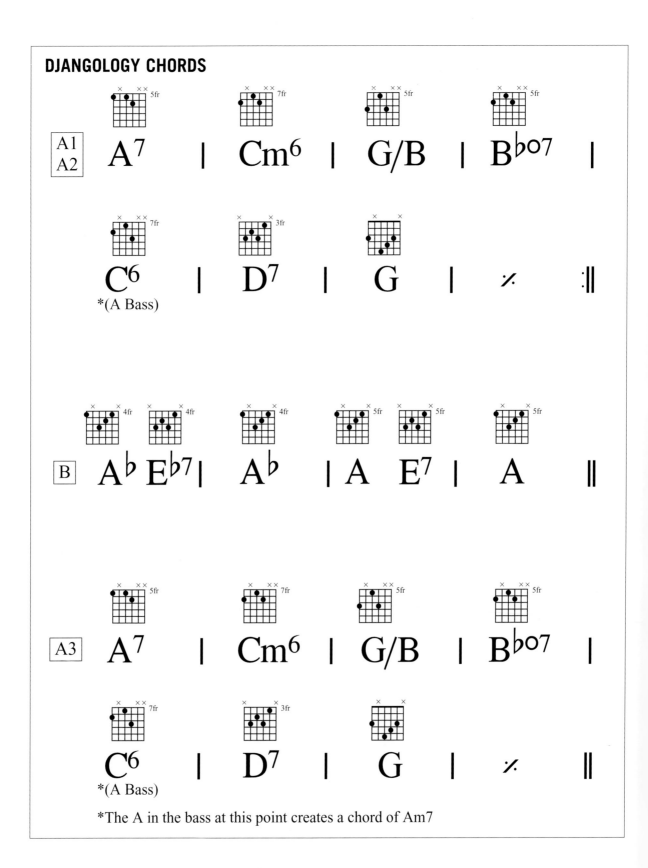

A1
A2

A^7 | Cm^6 | G/B | $B^{\flat o7}$ |

C^6 | D^7 | G | ⁄. :‖

*(A Bass)

B $A^\flat$ $E^{\flat 7}$| $A^\flat$ | A E^7 | A ‖

A3 A^7 | Cm^6 | G/B | $B^{\flat o7}$ |

C^6 | D^7 | G | ⁄. ‖

*(A Bass)

*The A in the bass at this point creates a chord of Am7

Sweet Chorus

Django plays a typically quirky solo introduction before bringing in the band for this slow tune in G major. There are fewer spectacular guitar gymnastics in this piece. And although there are some sections of fast arpeggios, Django prefers to elaborate on the bluesy chromaticism of the melody with frequent bends and intense vibrato.

STRUCTURE

After the intro there are just two choruses of the standard 32 bar 'AABA' form. Django plays the tune in the first chorus, taking the opportunity to improvise beautiful fills and flourishes whenever possible. The violin takes over the lead for the first two 'A' sections of the second chorus, with Django providing some of his trademark tremolando chords as accompaniment in bar 49. The second 'B' section involves both Stéphane and Django, but is in other respects a repeat of the first 'B' without the guitar fills. The final eight-bar 'A' is all violin, but it does give us an opportunity to examine Django's rhythm playing, and his striking rising arpeggios at the end as the rhythm guitars and bass drop out for the last three bars.

HARMONY

Django has once again come up with a distinctive chord structure, building tension as the minor 6th chords rise chromatically and then releasing it as the chords move to D7 and resolve to G. The 'B' section or bridge is a masterpiece of understatement, simply alternating between chords G and D7 (I and V7) before the conventional 'turnaround' of Em, A7 and D7, (or VI, II7 and V7). Notice the use of the dissonant sharpened fourth under the D7 chord here, balancing the sweetness of the melody with some more quirkiness.

The G major chords in the rhythm part are played using the left hand thumb over the neck to hold down the sixth string, leaving fingers one, two and three to fret the remaining notes; this is a common shape in hot club rhythm playing and well worth mastering as its sound is more transparent than the alternative full six-string bar chord. Django also uses this 'thumb-over' technique to hold down the sixth string for the G6/9 arpeggio at the end. He stops the fourth and fifth strings with his second finger, leaving the injured third and fourth fingers to hold down the top two strings; if you've ever wondered how he managed to play chords with only two undamaged fingers this is well worth studying.

MELODY

Both Reinhardt and Grappelli seem to have been aware that there was a unique quality to the melody of this piece, as they both remain faithful to its spirit throughout their respective choruses. Django still manages to fit in some glorious fills, such as the mandolin-style tremolando in bars 16/17 and the spectacular arpeggio-based re-interpretation of the tune from bar 38 to bar 40. He also seems to be able to come up with an endless variety of ways to decorate the opening 'bend' motif of the piece, adding extra notes or chromatic triplets each time it re-appears. Bars 31 to 33 are a good example of Django's use of three and four note chords to create melody; the E minor chord appears in several different inversions leading to the A9 shape, which is approached chromatically via a G#9.

RHYTHM

There is a good opportunity to hear the Hot Club piledriver effect in action in this tune. The rhythm guitars simply play the downbeats (with downstrokes) for much of the time, though occasionally the upbeats after the second and fourth beats are ghosted in with upstrokes. The bass plays 'twos'; ie, mostly only the first and third beats, though it's not uncommon to add a four beat line, particularly at the ends of sections. This sort of rhythm playing is an essential part of the authentic Hot Club style and close listening is highly recommended.

'Sweet Chorus' was the last of the six tracks recorded for the Gramophone label of France on October 15th 1936. It was one of two originals recorded that day: the other was the classic 'Swing Guitars'. Session records show that there was only one take, a sign of the relaxed confidence of the band under recording conditions. This was the year in which they undertook their first international tours, to Holland and Spain, and although the personnel was consistent on recording sessions and tours, jazz was still not that popular in France and work for the Quintette was intermittent. All the more remarkable, then, that their casual approach should produce a work of such beauty and depth.

(Tremolo pick slides)

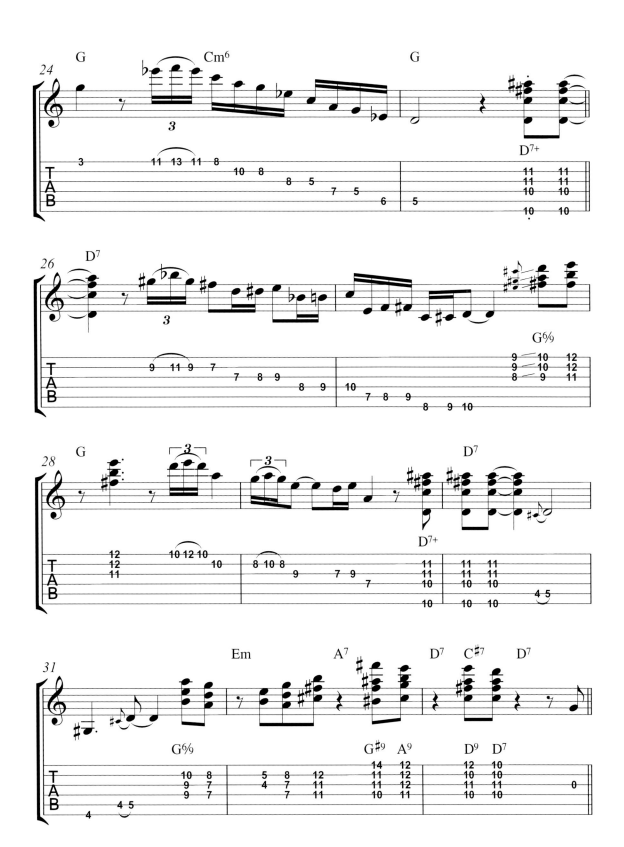

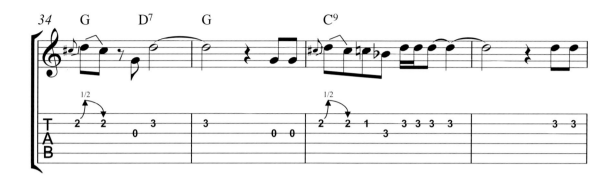

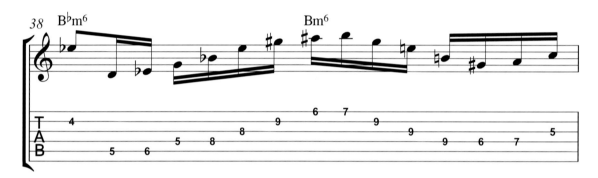

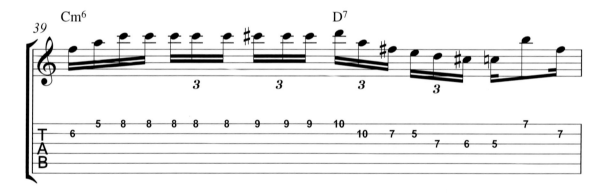

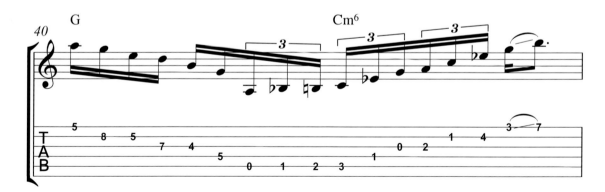

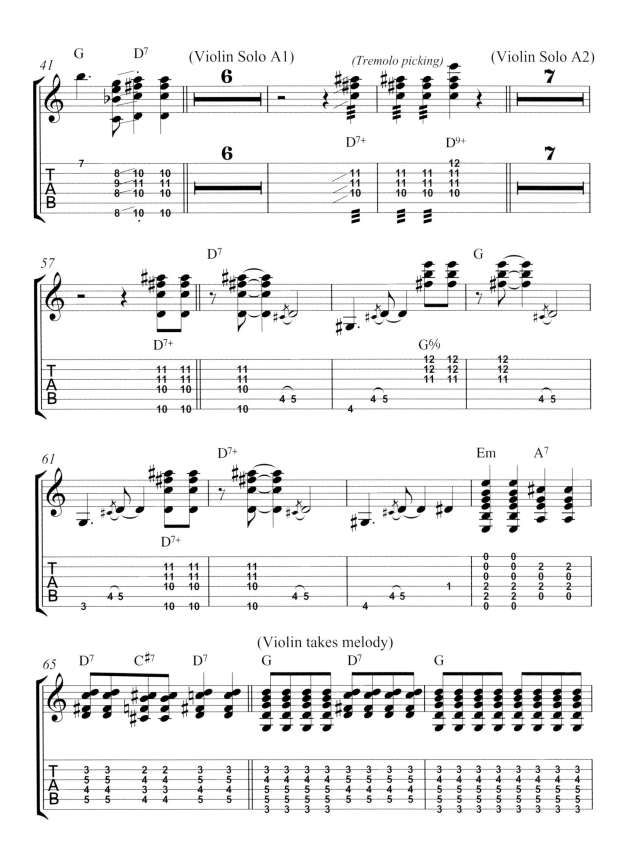

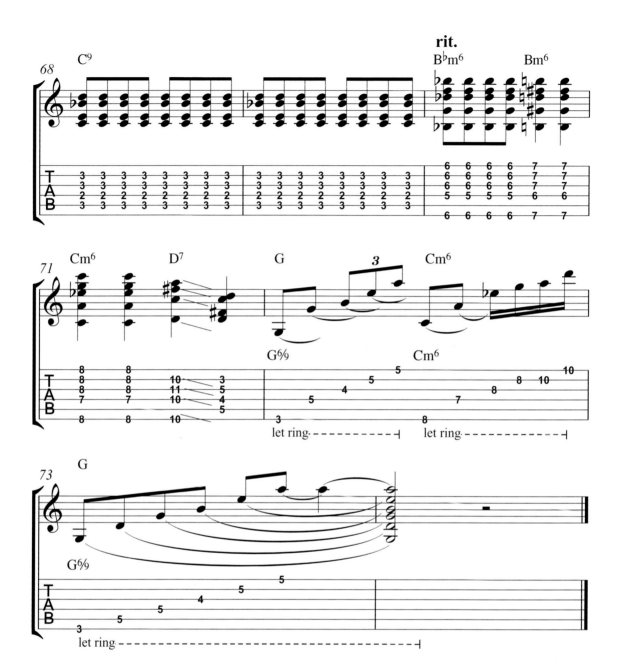

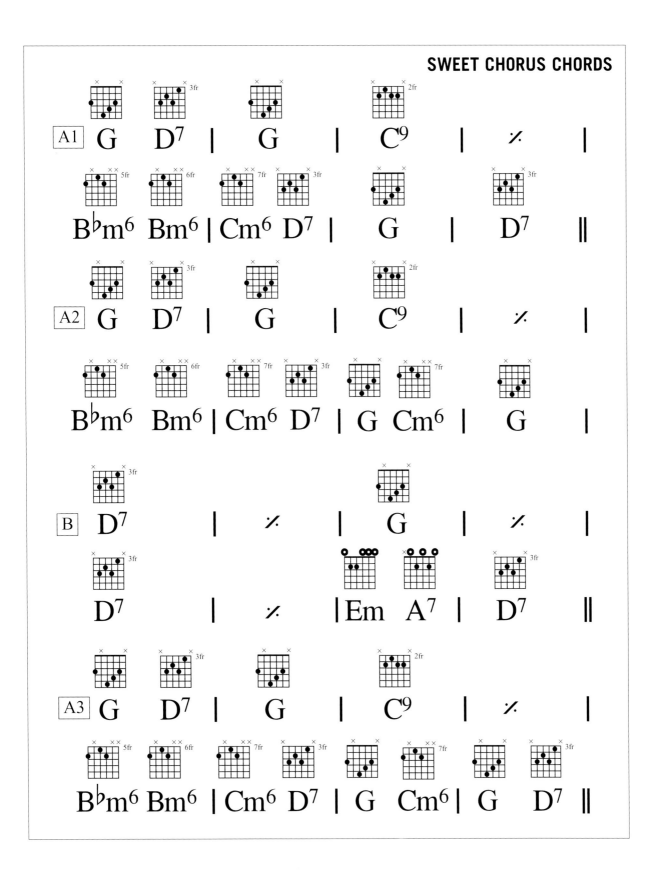

Bouncin' Around

This slow tune in G minor was written by the French trumpeter Gus Deloof and recorded in Paris on September 9th 1937 for the Swing label. It is not one of Django's most famous performances, yet it features some of his most technically brilliant and expressive playing. It also has a slimmed-down rhythm section, just one guitar and bass, which gives us the opportunity to hear the superb rhythm guitar of Louis Gasté uncluttered by other instruments.

INTRODUCTION

Django introduces the tune with some of his typically quirky arpeggios; a rising G minor is answered by a falling diminished 7th, then back to G minor, emphasising as so often the 6th of the chord, E. The C major 6th chord sounds strange, as the normal chord IV in this minor key would be C minor. The two bar pattern is then repeated, this time ending on a chord of D+ or D augmented, the dominant chord to G minor with the 5th sharpened. The song is a standard 32-bar form, AABA, and Django takes two choruses before finally returning to the introduction with a characteristic ending, again on a G minor 6th chord.

THE SOLO

The tune is played with typical flair and invention, using rapid decorative slurs, poignant bends and galloping arpeggios. There are also some amusing interjections, such as the open E and fretted E together in bar eight and the absurdly fast 'rakes' in bars 14 and 30. The fast chromatic run in bars 59 and 60 should be played with the first finger of the left hand, with a glissando-like action along the frets co-ordinated with extremely fast alternate picking from the right hand. This may take a great deal of practice, but it is possible! Notice also the change to a low register for the start of the second chorus, and the subsequent use of the very highest register in bar 61, a good example of Django's use of the whole guitar. Other key moments include Django's strident use of octaves in bars 43 and 44 (use only downstrokes with the pick to play these), some two-fret bends (eg, in bar 53) and the desolate sound of the tune played in parallel 4ths in the second chorus.

Rhythm and Harmony

The rhythm parts give us a chance to examine Django's favourite and most versatile chord. The same shape is used for both Gm6 and Am6. However, when used as Gm6 it is chord I, the key-chord or 'tonic' of the piece. When used as Am6 it is effectively chord V, the dominant chord. This is because this Am6 shape consists of the notes A, C and F#, the 5th (E) being omitted. The chord could be seen as D7, which should be D, F#, A and C, but in this case the root is omitted (in fact it is supplied by the double bass). The same shape is then used for Cm6, and can easily be added to in the 'middle-eight' or 'B' section to create F9 for the key change to Bb major.

Few of Django's contemporaries had such a grasp of guitar harmony that they could play most of a song with just one chord shape, and it maybe partly due to his injured left hand that he discovered and developed this technique. Django treats the first four bars of the solo as all Gm6, preferring to view the Am6 chord as a passing chord. For once there is a strong hint of 'blues scale' in much of the single note playing. He often uses a diminished arpeggio (F#, A, C and Eb) to suggest D7b9 over the next two bars (eg, bar 18), and this diminished flavouring peppers the whole piece.

On this session one other track was recorded, a classic rendition of 'St Louis Blues'. The two were released as A and B sides of a 78 rpm record for what was then the world's only dedicated jazz label. They wouldbe re-issued time and again on other labels.

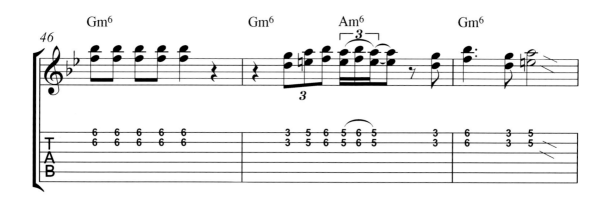

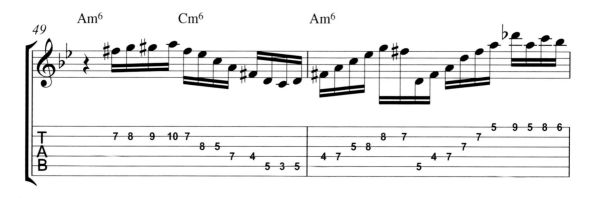

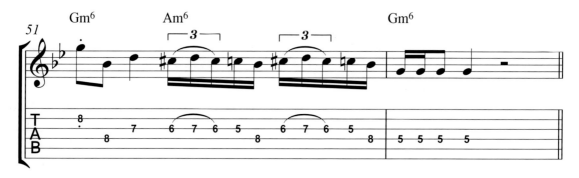

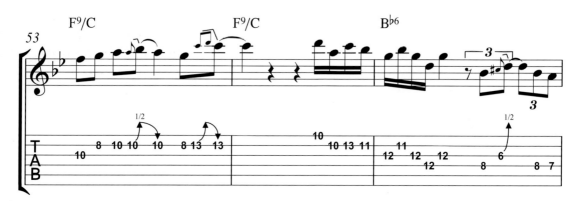

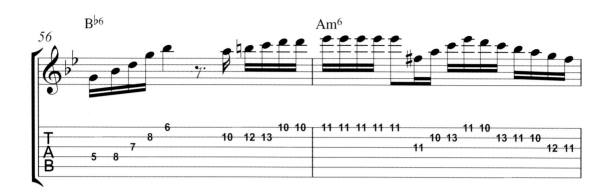

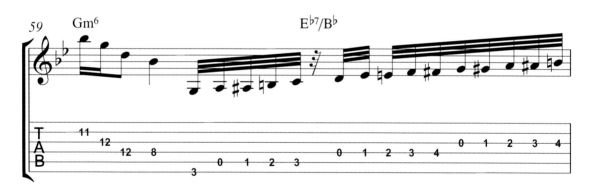

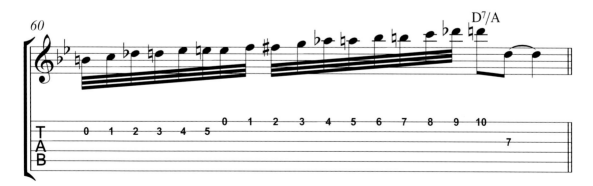

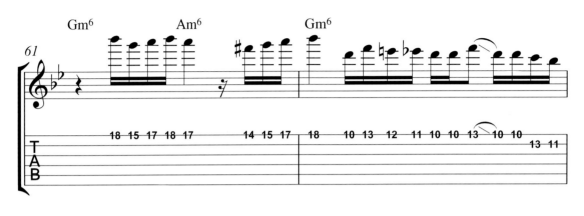

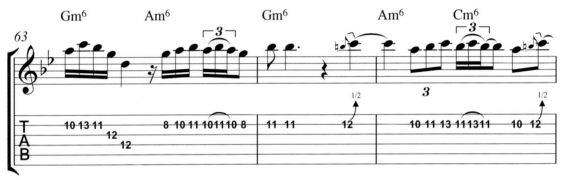

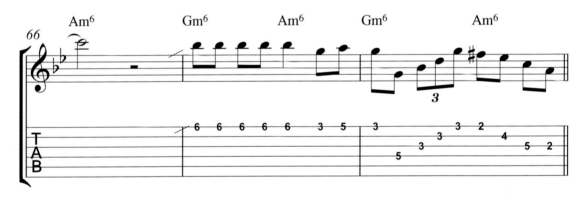

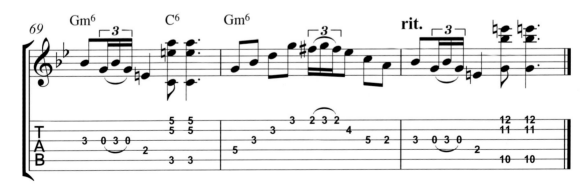

BOUNCIN' AROUND CHORDS

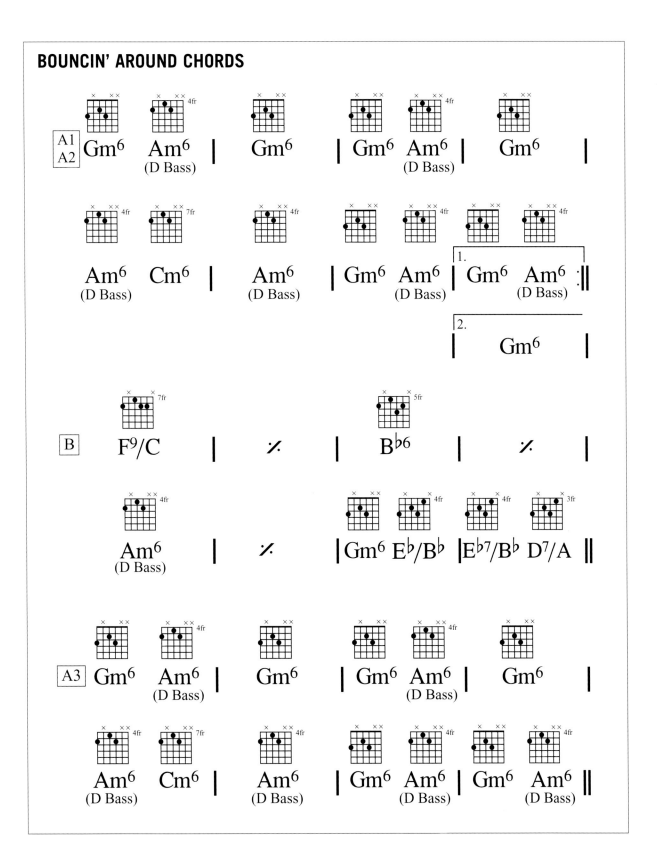

Minor Swing

Truly a Hot Club classic, this is arguably the most famous Reinhardt/Grappelli composition of them all. At first sight it appears to be a tune of remarkable simplicity. There is a chord sequence involving chords I, IV and V7 in A minor, (that's Am, Dm and E7) and a melody based on a rising arpeggio of each chord.

Look a little deeper and the form is not so straightforward: the theme is just eight bars long and played twice. Unusually, it is not re-stated at the end, there being a new 'riff' based eight-bar 'outro' with violin and guitar in unison, rather than in harmony as at the beginning. Neither of these two chord sequences is used for the solos, as guitar and violin take repeated choruses (four each) of a different sequence, 16 bars long this time. Nevertheless, the structural integrity of the whole piece is so strong that many musicians have played it without even realising they are using three different chord sequences!

INTRODUCTION

Django characteristically puts the minor 6th, B natural, in his D minor arpeggio that underpins Grappelli's. Other jazz musicians of the time would have favoured C, the 7th, but Django's Gypsy heritage seems to come through in the use of this 'darker' interval. Note also Django's typical use of a one-fret bend on the D minor chord, and that for once the bass player gets a moment to shine with two simple but classic fills.

RHYTHM GUITAR

The strumming pattern during the solos is slightly unusual here, the regulation Hot Club piledriver effect being abandoned for a more complex mix of a short downstroke on the first and third beats, with an accented downstroke on beats two and four, and a lighter upstroke on the following quavers. The resulting 'chack changa-chack' may need careful practice from even the most seasoned Hot Club aficionados.

THE SOLO

Django's dramatic chordal entry involves the use of his third and fourth fingers; obviously not a problem when playing chords. The first note of the following pull-off is also likely to be played with finger four; it seems Django could use his injured fingers for single notes if he wished, though mainly on the E and B strings. Harmonically speaking, many trademarks can be found. The guitarist avoids the more common 'jazzy' Dorian mode and instead goes for the dramatic-sounding harmonic minor scale. He also uses the diminished 7th chord built on G# to play over the E7 chord, creating a harmony consisting of E, G#, B, D and F, which make an E7b9 chord. Typically, we find the 6th, B, used on the D minor chord and its counterpart F# used on the A minor chord.

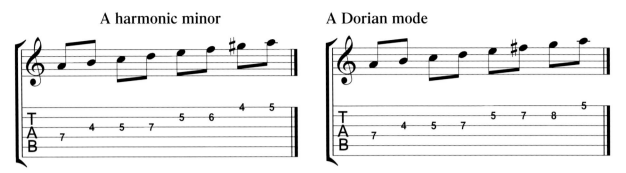

A harmonic minor   A Dorian mode

There are a few things in this solo that will cause even the most technically competent guitarist to break into a sweat. The 'swept' arpeggio in bar 36, the frequent bends and glisses, and the rapid arpeggios are standard stuff for Django, as is the chromatic scale, probably played with one left hand finger, in bars 44 to 46. The tremolando chord slide from the 10th fret to the 15th and back down to the 3rd may cause problems, however: try getting the right hand up to speed on its own, first. And the following fast chromatic scale in triplets, with an even faster arpeggio at the end, may induce frustration and resignation in equal measure.

The band recorded four tracks during the November 25th 1937 session that included 'Minor Swing', three of which were Reinhardt/Grappelli compositions. Before the end of the year they had recorded seven more original compositions in various line-ups, ranging from 13-piece band to the usual quintet. This was one of the most fruitful periods for Django, and clearly composition had become a significant part of his creative life.

Violin arranged for Guitar (Stephane Grappelli)

Guitar (Django Reinhardt)

(Chords implied by harmony)

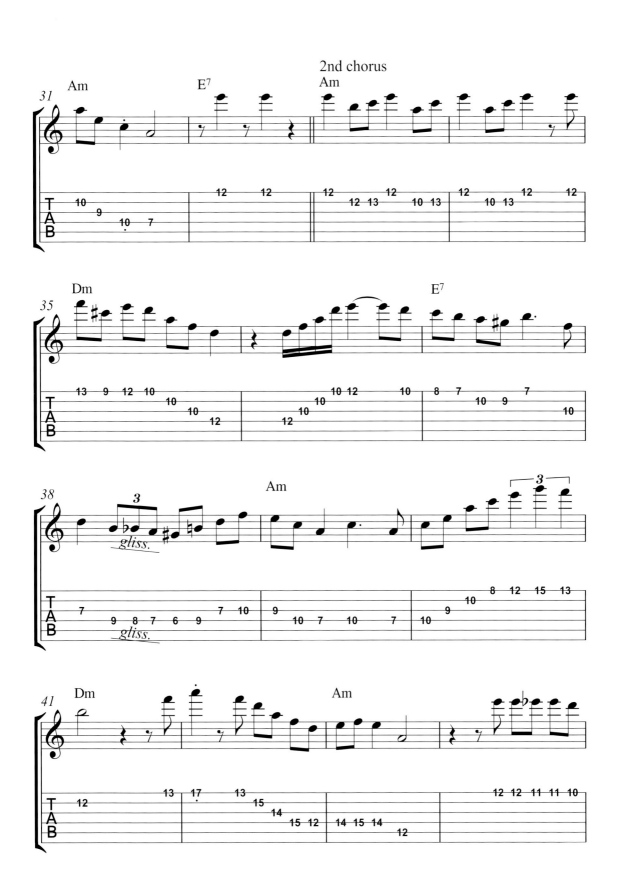

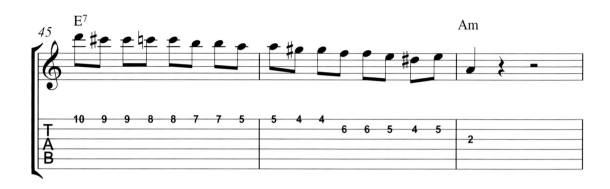

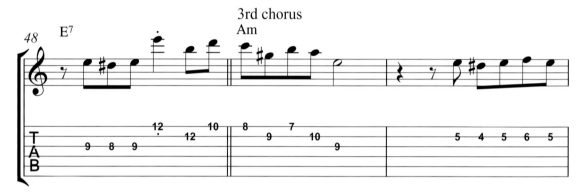

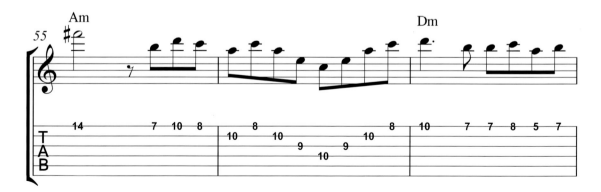

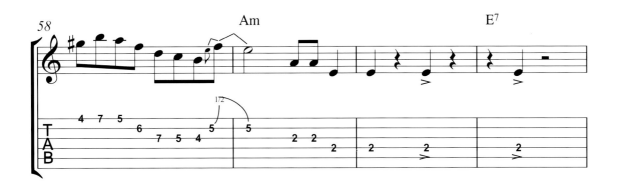

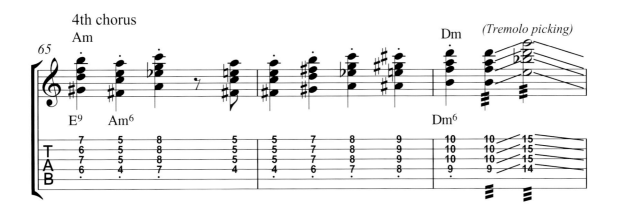

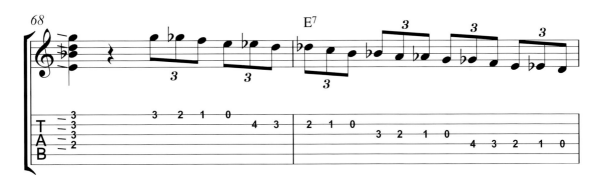

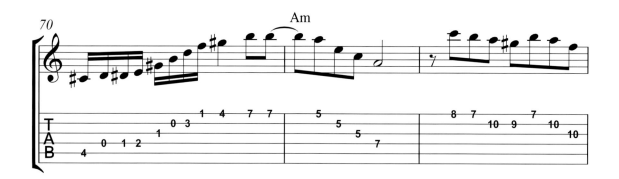

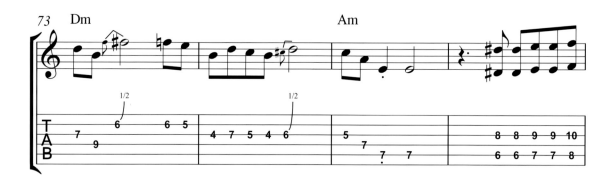

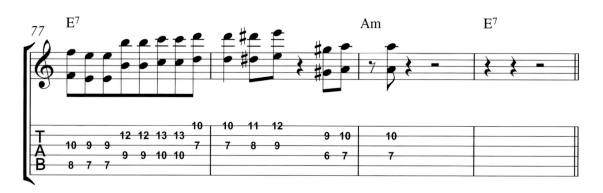

MINOR SWING CHORDS

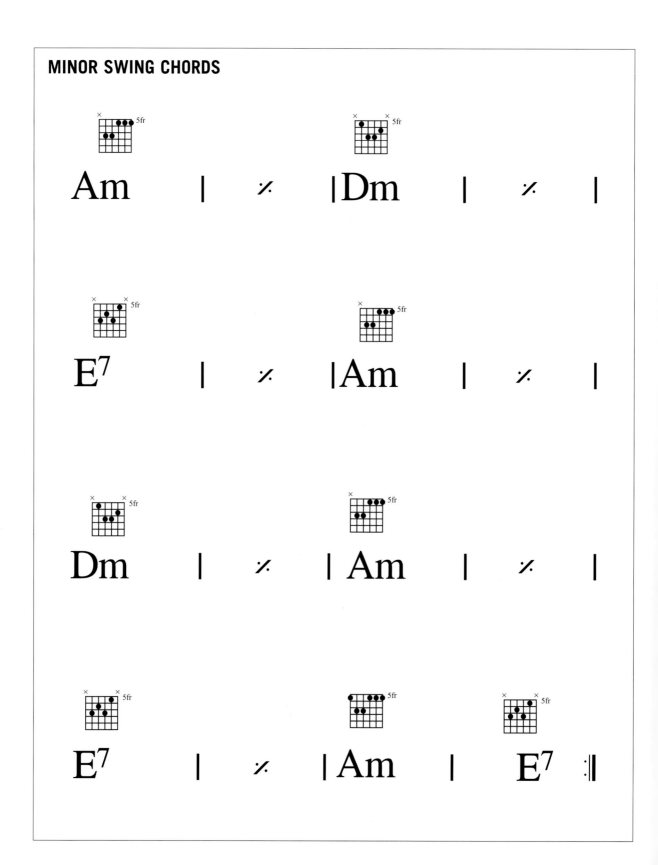

Honeysuckle Rose

This recording was made at Decca recording studios in London, at the start of one of the Quintette's most successful tours of England, where the band so often received a rapturous welcome. The melody of 'Honeysuckle Rose' would have been well known to audiences in the 1930s so the Quintette du Hot Club de France approach the song with characteristic freedom, and Django prefers to quote only the opening bars of the vocal refrain before launching into his solo. First, however, we are treated to a riff-based introduction with a blues-tinged flavour played in harmony by Django and Stéphane Grappelli.

STRUCTURE
The song follows the standard jazz-tune 'AABA' format of four eight-bar sections, making 32 bars altogether, preceeded by an eight-bar introduction in which the violin and guitar play in harmony. Django takes the first two choruses and there is then one chorus of Stéphane Grappelli's violin. In the fourth and final chorus, violin and guitar play a riff similar to the intro over the A sections, and, urged on by Django, Stéphane solos on the last B section. The intro is then used as the outro, bringing the arrangement to a satisfying symmetrical conclusion.

THE SOLO
The first two bars of Django's solo quote the melody of the song, but from there on he improvises freely, and occasionally playfully, over the harmonically straightforward changes. He plays a cute chromatic line in bars 19-21, and avoids being bogged-down in the otherwise simple harmony by using devices like a Gdim7 arpeggio in bar 23, even though the underlying chord is F major. This chord is one of Django's favourite tricks. Gdim7 consists of G, Bb, Db and E (or to be precise, Fb), which can be reorganised into a chord of C7b9 with the root omitted: C,E,G,Bb and Db. He is therefore playing over the F major chord with a C7b9 arpeggio. A similar diminished arpeggio can be found over C7 in bar 45, (starting on C# this time) and over F7 in bar 59.

In bar 43 there is a different use of a diminished arpeggio as Cdim is played over a C7 chord. This arpeggio gives the root (C), the #9th (Eb or D#), the #11th (F#) and the 13th (A) and thus contains most of the dissonant, more interesting notes of an extended dominant chord. Notice how Django also delays the resolution of this C7 line to F major, as in bar 46 he continues with C7 harmony even though the chords have moved on to F. All in all he is able to mix up chromatic lines, arpeggios, and octave passages into a seamless whole as though every note was in place before he even began to play.

RHYTHM
The rhythm guitars play Hot Club at its simplest; downstrokes on the downbeats, slightly staccato and with beats two and four slightly accented. This is the most common approach to Hot Club rhythm and grew out of the swing feel found in the rhythm

sections of bands of the 1920s, such as Duke Ellington or Louis Armstrong.

Django is such a great player that it is easy to lose sight of the importance of the ensemble playing in these tracks. We take it for granted that the band is 'tight', but we should notice the lively bounce of the rhythm section and the originality of the arrangement in the intro and outro (often copied note for note by Hot Club-inspired bands the world over). Add the subtle blues-inflected swing of Stéphane Grappelli and Django's relaxed and inventive solo and once again we have a classic. This was the first of eight tracks recorded on January 31st 1938. The others include exemplary renditions of the standards 'Sweet Georgia Brown' and 'Night and Day', and no fewer than five Reinhardt/Grappelli originals. A good day's work.

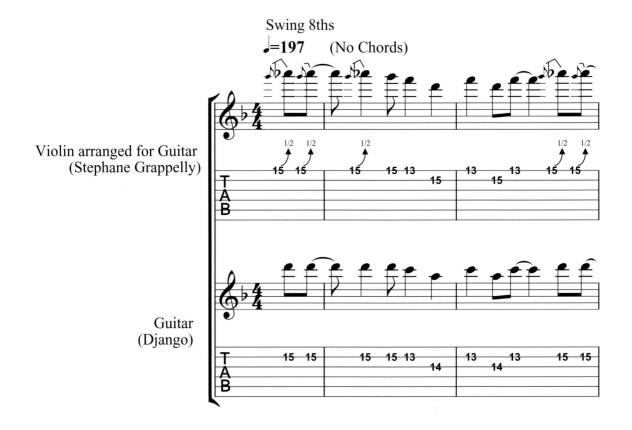

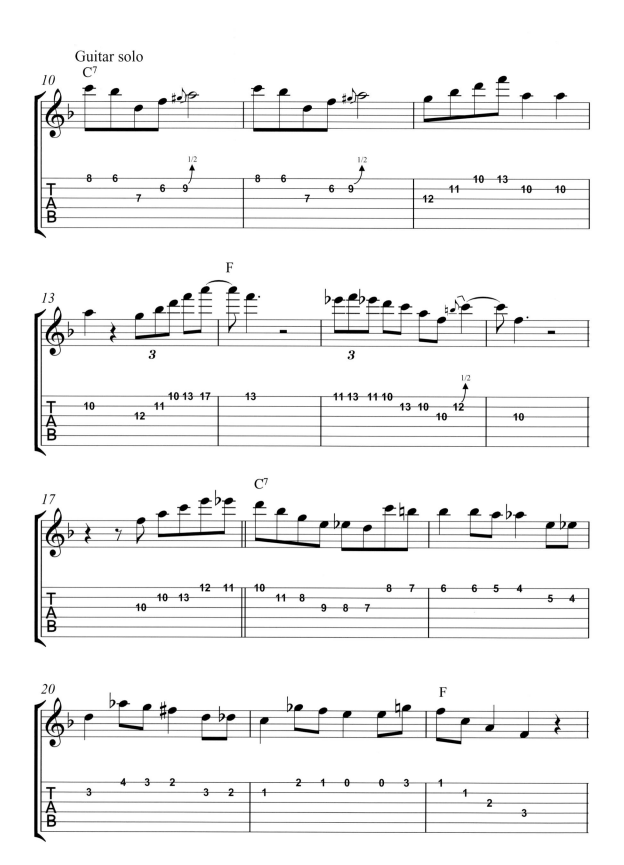

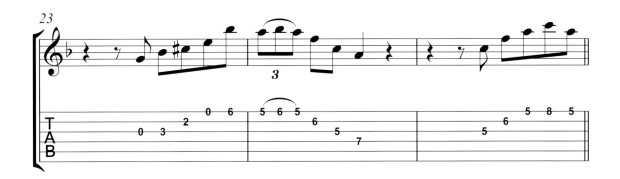

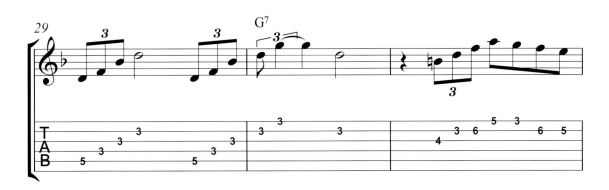

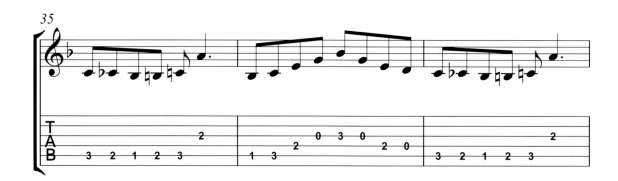

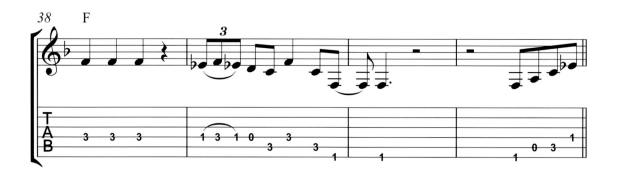

2nd chorus

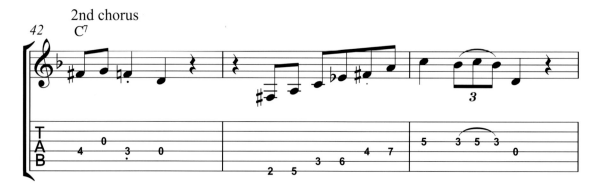

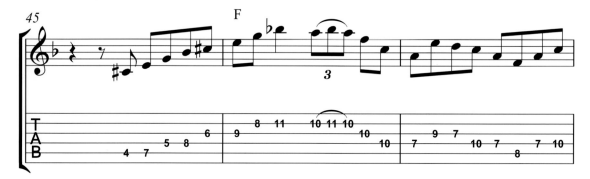

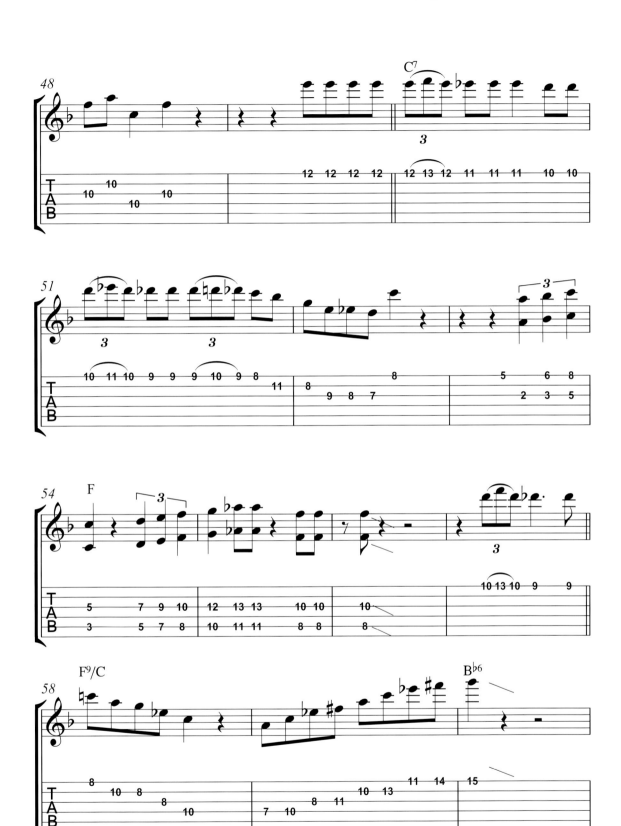

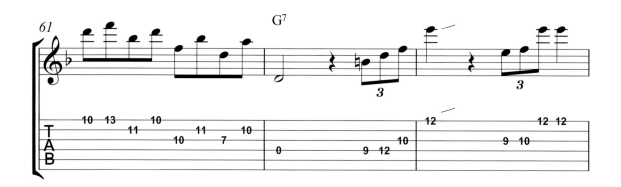

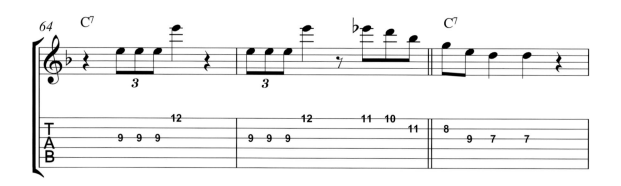

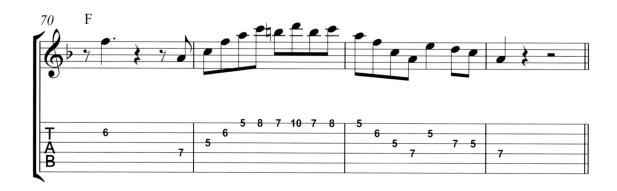

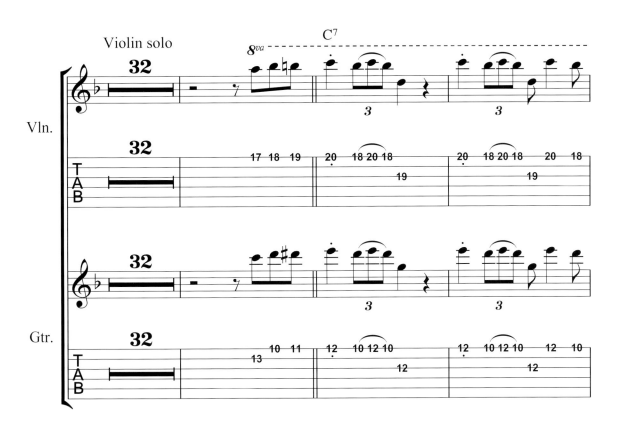

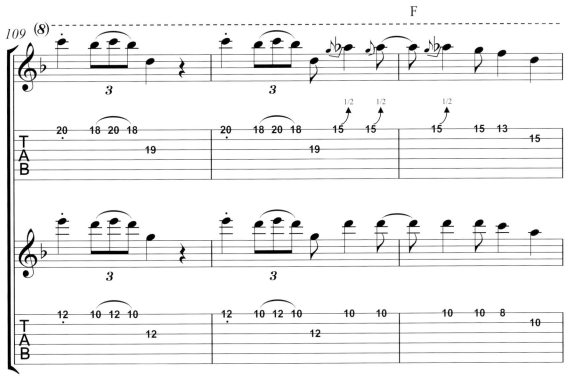

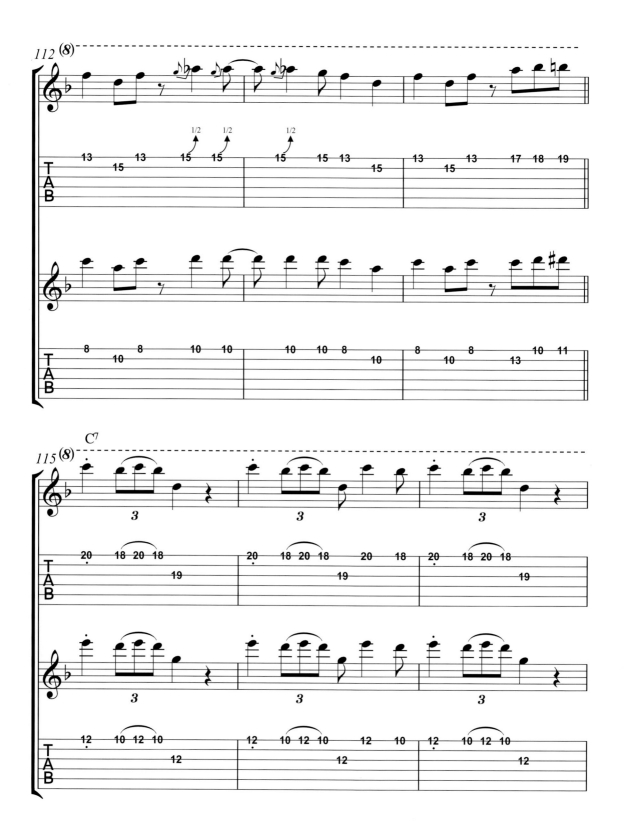

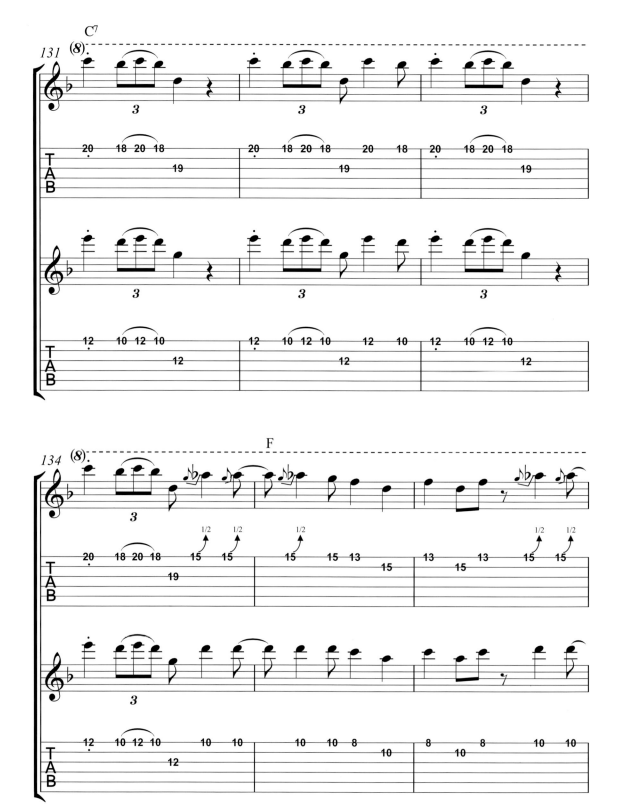

HONEYSUCKLE ROSE CHORDS

A1 C7 | ⁒ | ⁒ | ⁒ |
F | ⁒ | ⁒ | ⁒ ||
A2 C7 | ⁒ | ⁒ | ⁒ |
F | ⁒ | ⁒ | ⁒ ||
7fr
6fr
B F9/C | ⁒ | B♭6 | ⁒ |
G7 | ⁒ | C7 | ⁒ ||
A3 C7 | ⁒ | ⁒ | ⁒ |
F | ⁒ | ⁒ | ⁒ ||

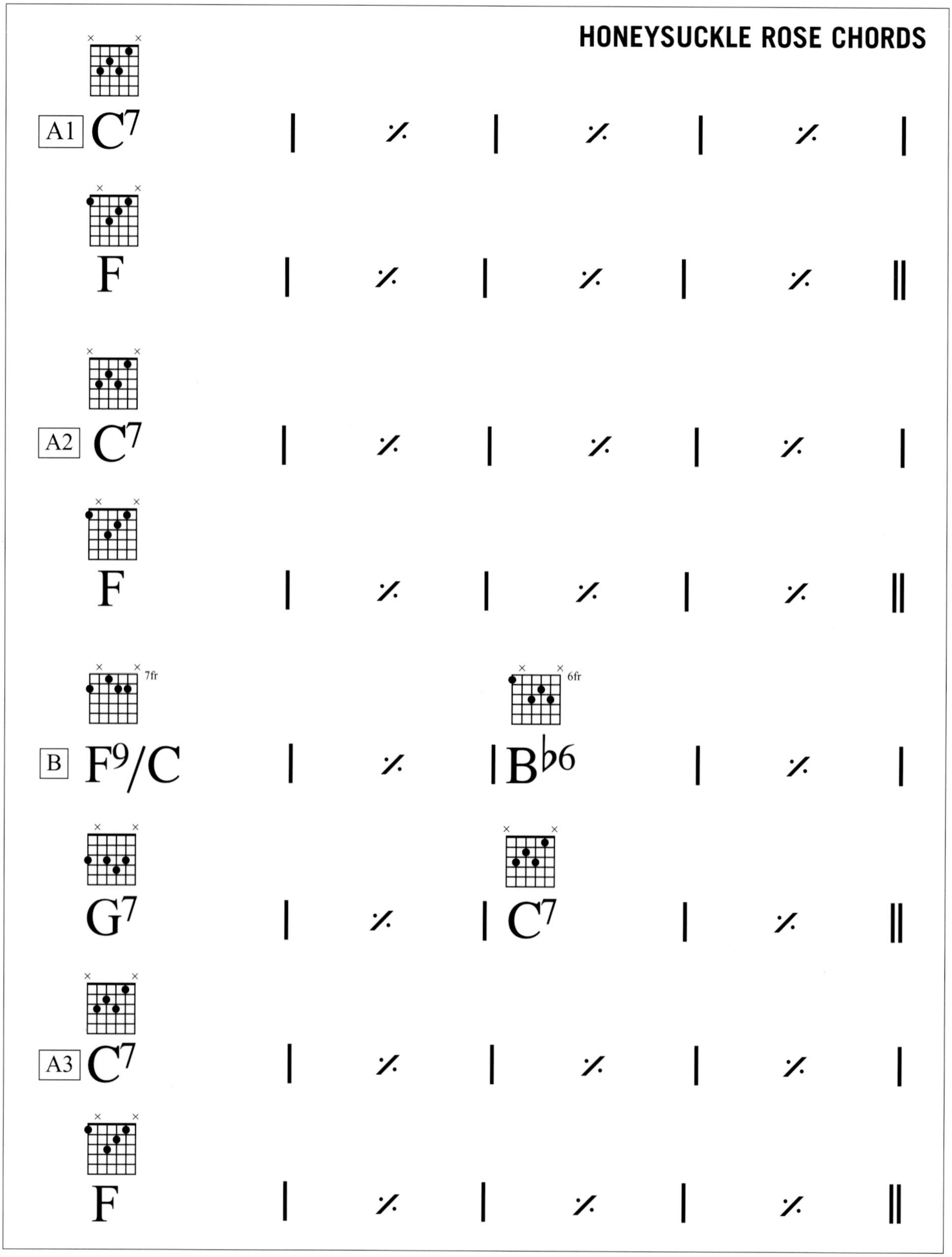

Nuages

With the outbreak of war, in 1939, Stéphane Grappelli stayed in England, where the Quintette du Hot Club de France had been on tour, whilst Django hurried back across the Channel to Paris. Gradually over the next few months he formed a new Quintette, with a sound more clearly influenced by the American jazz of Benny Goodman. Gone were the second rhythm guitarist and the violin, and in their place came the drums of Pierre Fouad and the clarinet of Hubert Rostaing.

With the fall of Paris and the German occupation came a thirst, in France, for the freedom associated with all things American. Django could hardly have been better placed, and was in great demand as a performer and recording artist.

'Nuages' was first recorded with the band's regular instrumentation on October 1st 1940, but the record, though only slightly different in form from the version heard here, was never issued. On December 13th 1940, Django and his new group tried again, this time with the addition of a second clarinet, played by Alix Combelle. The record was an instant success, has become an icon of French jazz, and is Django's most famous composition.

INTRODUCTION

The track begins with a scurrying, edgy introduction, first centred on B9, then sliding chromatically up a step to C9, with the first clarinet providing the tension through a riff using the flattened 5th of these chords. The solo clarinet then brings in the melody over an implied Db7, the contrast with the intro made more dramatic by the rest of the band joining in a bar later as the harmony moves through Gdim, C7 and finally to the home chord of F major.

Progressions using variations of II, V, I are common in jazz, but here the II chord is substituted by a dominant built on the bVI, allowing Django to create an unusually chromatic melody. The fact that Django does not himself play the melody is no disadvantage to us, as we have a chance to hear his delightful fills and tremolandos behind Rostaing's expressive playing; both are transcribed, so you have the full picture.

Interestingly, this version of 'Nuages' is slower than the earlier one, adding to the ominous portent of the introduction, and the extra clarinet allows for a thicker texture both here and on the later big-band inspired riff section.

STRUCTURE

Though the melody of 'Nuages' is 32 bars in length, the commonplace AABA form is not used here, as each eight-bar section is different from the others, giving us a form best represented as ABCD. The only repeated material is found in the A section, which is made up of two identical four-bar phrases. This same four-bar phrase also makes up the second half of the D section, though altered to bring the melody to a close. The structure of the whole track is even more complex, as we shall see.

SOLO

Django's solo begins with artificial harmonics; the left hand frets the note as usual, but the right hand thumb plucks the string whilst the index finger touches it 12 frets above the fretted note. Some players sound the harmonic with the pick by holding it between thumb and middle finger and again using the index finger on the octave; there may be other ways: experiment and see which works best for you. The resultant sound is one octave higher than written, with a charming, bell-like quality. There is also a natural, 12th fret harmonic to be found in bar 55, as Django punctuates a long, fluid phrase with a brief moment of added sparkle.

RIFFS

The solo is followed by a great piece of arranging. Instead of re-stating the tune, as so often happens after the solos in a jazz record, the two clarinets and Django's guitar join in three-part harmony to play a riff based on the chords of the opening four bars. Essentially Django has shared out the three-note chords that he might have played on the guitar between the three musicians to excellent effect. These chords, and Django's thinking, can be seen below:

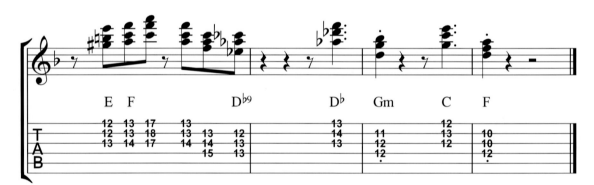

For the next section the form is now shortened slightly, the B section and first four bars of C being omitted, as the clarinets play in thirds on the second half of C and Django plays rhythm. For the first half of D the roles are reversed as the clarinets play a sustained supporting figure and the guitar plays a variation of the melody, before the solo clarinet returns to finish the tune accompanied by Django's arpeggios and final chordal comments.

With 'Nuages', Django came up with a beautiful and classic melody, a startling and original introduction and a solo of typical inventiveness. He also managed to include an interesting piece of harmony writing for guitar and two clarinets and to maintain interest by tinkering with the form. At this point in his career Django's mastery of composition and arranging as well as of the guitar could hardly be more clearly demonstrated.

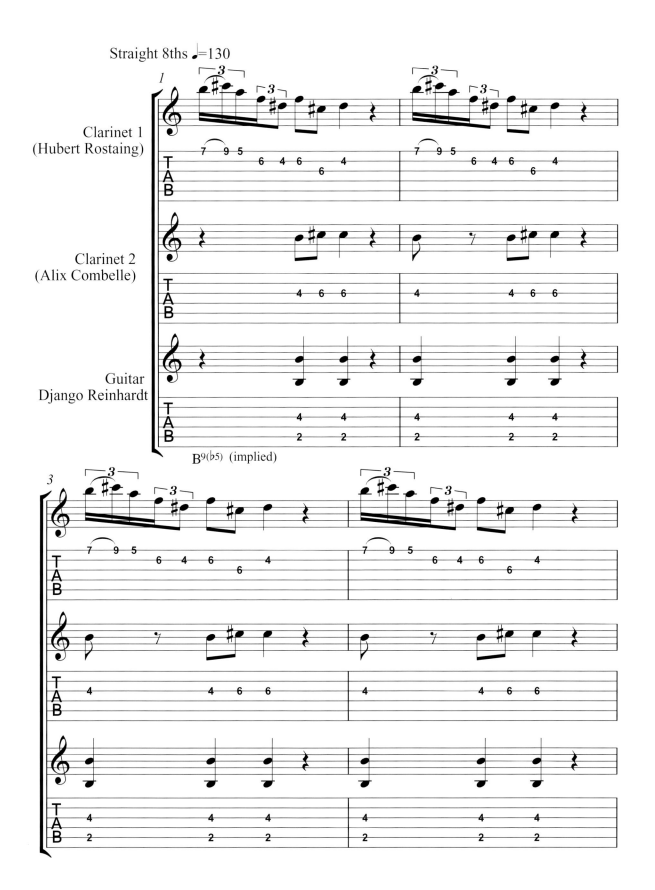

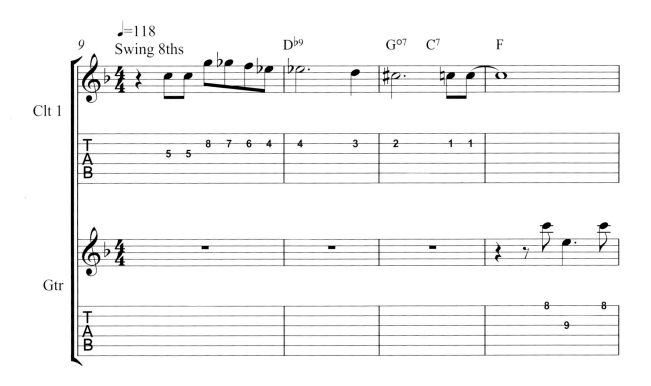

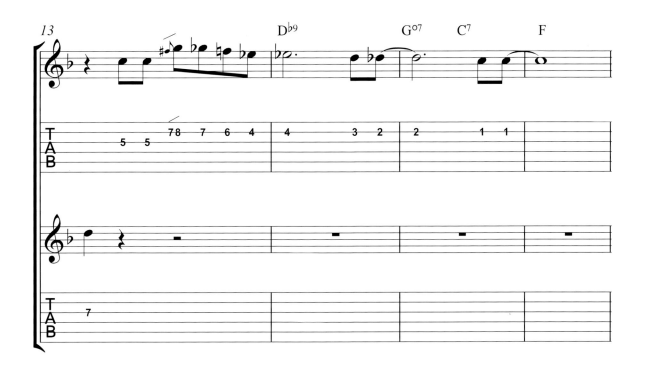

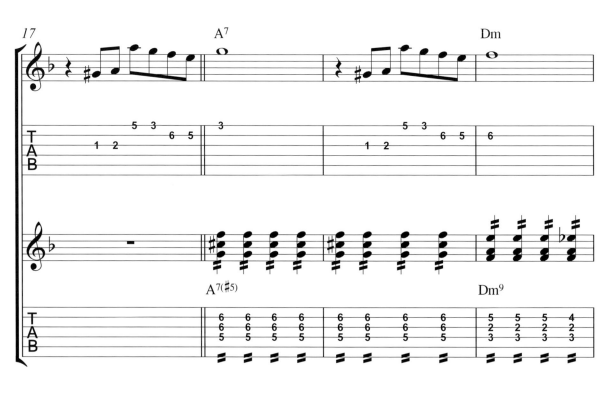

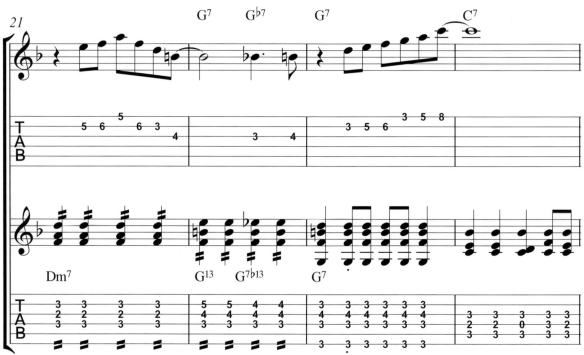

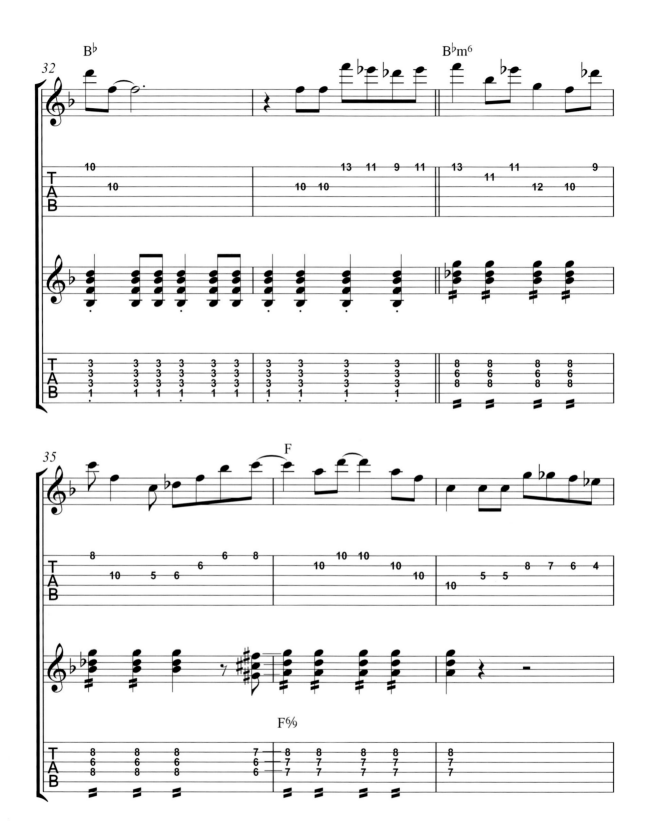

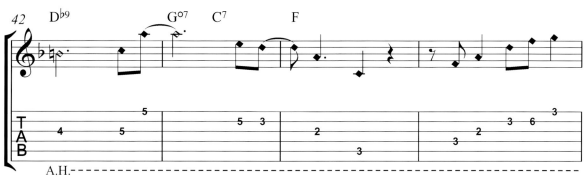

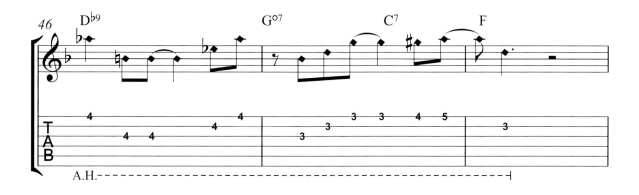

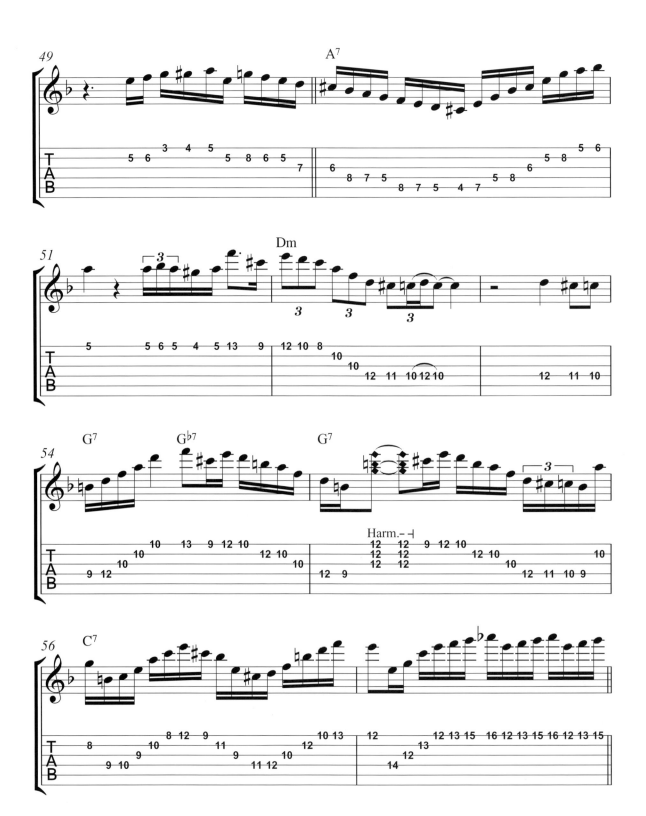

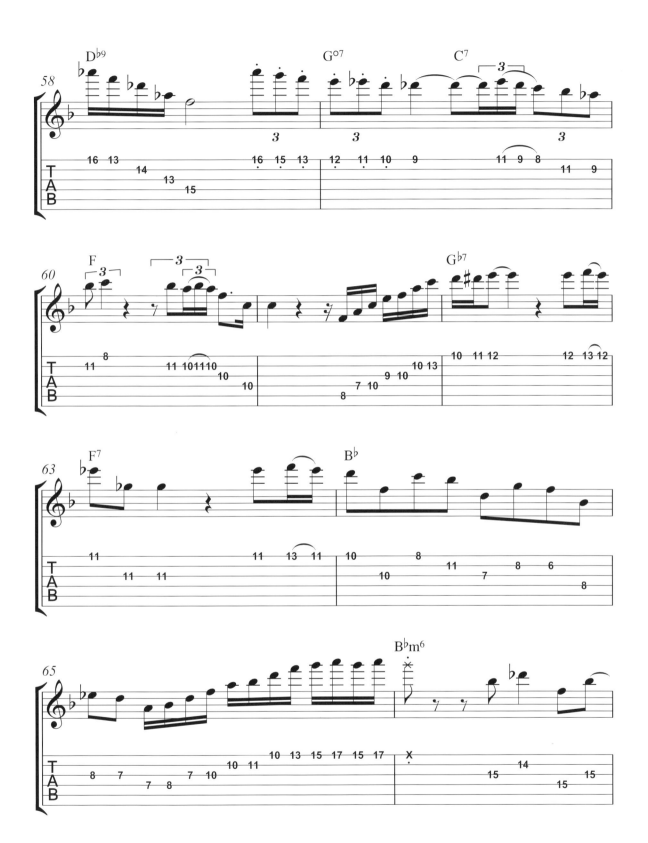

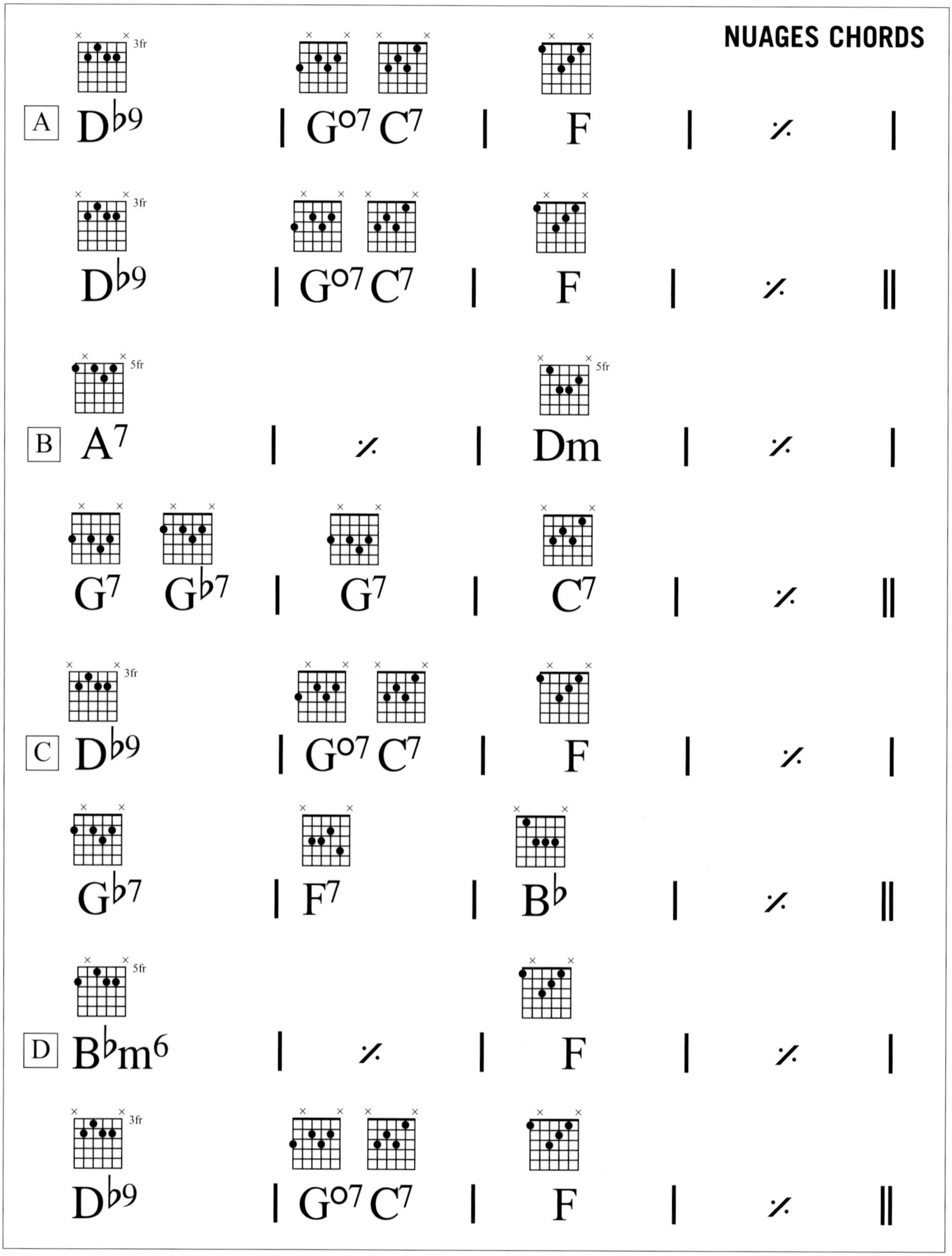

NUAGES CHORDS

A D^{b9} | $G^{o7} C^7$ | F | ∕. |

D^{b9} | $G^{o7} C^7$ | F | ∕. ‖

B A^7 | ∕. | Dm | ∕. |

G^7 G^{b7} | G^7 | C^7 | ∕. ‖

C D^{b9} | $G^{o7} C^7$ | F | ∕. |

G^{b7} | F^7 | B^b | ∕. ‖

D B^bm^6 | ∕. | F | ∕. |

D^{b9} | $G^{o7} C^7$ | F | ∕. ‖

140

On the CD

The CD contains recordings of the six Django Reinhardt transcriptions in this book, including lead guitar, two rhythm guitars and bass. They are modelled on available Django recordings you can track down using the session dates and catalogue numbers.

The CD was recorded using a technique known as 'middle and side', in which a pair of 'figure of eight' microphones are fixed at right-angles. A Coles 4040 ribbon mic facing into the room captured the 'middle' image, while a Coles 4038 provided the 'side' or left and right images, allowing control over stereo width.

Rod Fogg played all the parts, beginning with rhythm guitar one, to the right of the mics. He then moved to the left side to play rhythm guitar two, then added bass, in the centre and back from the mics. Finally the lead (Django) parts were played in mono immediately in front of the Coles 4040. The recordings capture the acoustic effect of musicians grouped together around a microphone in a live room, as in the original Hot Club recordings, but allow the prominence of the lead guitar and the degree of stereo spread to be determined at mixdown. This method was devised by Huw Price, who recorded, mixed and co-produced the CD with Rod Fogg.

TRACK 1: TUNING TONES

TRACK 2: 'DJANGOLOGY' (Reinhardt, Grappelli)
Based on P77540, recorded September 1935 by Django Reinhardt, guitar; Stéphane Grappelli, violin; Joseph Reinhardt and Pierre Ferret, rhythm guitars; Louis Vola, bass.

TRACK 3: 'SWEET CHORUS' (Reinhardt, Grappelli)
Based on OLA 1295-1, recorded October 15th 1936 with the same line-up.

TRACK 4: 'BOUNCIN' AROUND' (Gus Deloof)
Based on OLA 1953-1, recorded September 9th 1937 by Django Reinhardt, guitar; Louis Gasté, rhythm guitar; Eugène d'Hellemmes, bass.

TRACK 5: 'MINOR SWING' (Reinhardt, Grappelli)
Based on OLA 1990-1, recorded November 25th 1937 by Django Reinhardt, guitar; Stéphane Grappelli, violin; Joseph Reinhardt and Pierre Ferret, rhythm guitars; Louis Vola, bass.

TRACK 6: 'HONEYSUCKLE ROSE' (Waller/Razaf)
Based on DTB3523-1, recorded January 31st 1938 by Django Reinhardt, guitar; Stéphane Grappelli, violin; Roger Chaput and Eugene Vées, rhythm guitars; Louis Vola, bass.

TRACK 7: 'NUAGES' (Reinhardt)
Based on OSW146-1, recorded December 13th 1940 by Django Reinhardt, guitar; Joseph Reinhardt, rhythm guitar; Hubert Rostaing, clarinet; Alix Combelle, clarinet; Tony Rovira, bass; Pierre Fouad, drums.

Bibliography

Many books and articles on the subject of Django, the Hot Club Quintette and Gipsy jazz in general have been published over the years in several languages. The following are particularly interesting.

Django Reinhardt by Charles Delaunay (Ashley Mark, 1981)
English translation of a memoir by the French critic and co-founder of the Hot Club de France, who knew Django throughout his career. Too anecdotal to be a true biography, but full of interest.

Django's Gypsies by Ian Cruickshank (Ashley Mark, 1994)
Subtitled 'The mystique of Django Reinhardt and his People', this collection of memorabilia,

quotations, press cuttings and photographs presents a vivid picture of Django's world, then and now.

Stéphane Grappelli by Geoffrey Smith (Pavilion / Michael Joseph 1987)
Exemplary biography of Django's long-time partner, with a great deal about Django himself.

La Tristesse de Saint Louis by Michael Zwerin (Quartet, 1985)
The subtitle, 'Swing Under the Nazis', describes the contents perfectly.

Jazz Away From Home by Chris Goddard (Paddington Press, 1979)
The early impact of jazz on Europe, particularly France.

NOTE
The term Gipsy (or Gypsy) is frowned upon in some quarters nowadays, and the word Roma is coming more into favour. I have stuck to Gipsy, not out of disrespect but because Roma has not yet attained universal currency and may not be understood by some readers.

To learn more about today's flourishing Gipsy-jazz scene, try **www.jazzpartout.com** or, if you have plenty of time, just type "Django Reinhardt" or "Hot Club" into your search engine. The amount of material, in English, French, German, Dutch, etc, is quite astonishing.

Suggested recordings

Django's recordings are constantly being compiled, released, deleted and repackaged by record labels around the world. Because of this, it is impossible to draw up a permanent, definitive list of the best available selection. The material listed below was all current in June 2004, and advertised on at least one of the big mail-order websites.

Single CD compilations
Quintessential: Le Quintette du Hot Club de France 25 Classics 1934-40
ASV Living Era 5267
(A well-chosen selection from the classic period.)

Djangology (1934-35)
Naxos 8120515
(The first 18 released tracks by the Quintette. The following two Naxos CDs cover the rest of the original Quintette's life.)

Swing Guitars (1936-37)
Naxos 8120686

HCQ Strut (1938-39)
Naxos 8128707

All-Star Sessions
Blue Note 31577
(Includes music from Rex Stewart and
Coleman Hawkins sessions.)

Double-CD packs
Pêche à la Mouche
Verve 835 418-2
(Post-war recordings, including the complete
March 1953 Blue Star album.)

Gipsy Jazz School: Django's Legacy
Iris Music 3001 845
(Fascinating collection containing a few
Django tracks alongside a wonderful parade of
material by other Gipsy jazz guitarists –
Ferret, Vées, Rosenberg, Joseph and Babik

Reinhardt – and even a short 1952 radio
interview with Django himself.)

Four-CD boxes
Django 50th Anniversary Memorial
EPM 160292
(French anthology featuring two CDs by the
original Quintette and one each from the
wartime and post-war periods.)

Django & his American Friends 1934-45
Definitive 11167
(Sessions featuring Coleman Hawkins, Dicky
Wells, Rex Stewart, Larry Adler, Glenn Miller
sidemen – 101 tracks in all.)

Swing de Paris
Proper PROPERBX 53
(No fewer than 103 tracks, from the rejected
("too modern") Odeon session of 1934 to the
Club St Germain quintet of 1952. A good
selection representing every phase.)

Acknowledgements

Many kind and generous offers of help were received during the making of this book; please
accept my thanks and apologies if I have missed you from this list.

For the loan of guitars, and valuable background information on Selmers: Nils Solberg and
Rebecca Brown; Roger Pearce; Wunjo Guitars, London (www.wunjoguitars.com); Bill Puplett.

For recording the CD: Huw Price.

For his essential book, *The Story of Selmer-Maccaferri Guitars*: François Charle
(www.lutherie.net).

Dave Alexander (www.hotclub.co.uk).

Strings by Newtone Strings (www.newtonestrings.com). Guitars by John Le Voi
(www.levoi.freeserve.co.uk).

Visit www.rodfogg.com for more on playing Django Reinhardt.

Index